New Tools
for Learning

Accelerated
learning
meets ICT

John Davitt ■

Published by Network Educational Press Ltd
PO Box 635
Stafford
ST16 1BF

First published 2005
© John Davitt 2005

ISBN 1 85539 131 7

Every effort has been make to contact copyright holders of material reproduced in this book. The publishers apologize for any omissions and will be pleased to rectify them at the earliest opportunity. Please see page 131 for a comprehensive list of acknowledgements.

Managing Editor: Sarah Nunn
Technical Editor: Mike Bostock
Cover design: Neil Hawkins, NEP
Layout: Marc Maynard, NEP
Illustrator: Katherine Baxter (pages 9, 13, 23, 53, 68, 69, 73, 78, 85, 89, 97, 121, 123, 125)
Illustrator: Spike Gerrell (pages 28, 29, 37, 42, 49, 87, 101)

Printed in Great Britain by MPG Books Ltd, Bodmin, Cornwall

Contents

Foreword

I have had the great honour and pleasure to travel a lot of the world for over a decade talking, advising and consulting about ICT and learning. It is a personal passion and, being married to a teacher, an issue that concerns me both professionally and personally. When I started I met many enthusiasts who shared a dream that we could use ICT to transform the experience of education and deliver a global aspiration of education for every citizen of the world. Against these lofty ambitions the perennial constraints of budgets, political will and professional inertia were easily visible. There were many fears expressed to me. Most importantly, there was a concern that, somehow, ICT would be used as an excuse to sack teachers and close schools and pump learning into kids' heads through impersonal technology.

Being an optimist, my experience over the last decade has kept those lofty aspirations alive. It has also made the fundamental truths about both education and learning clear to me. First, learning is at its heart a social and a socializing experience. ICTs are very powerful tools, but smart technologies need smart people, they don't replace them. In a world where technology is increasingly pervasive, teachers become more not less important.

Second, as the world becomes increasingly connected, as technology and science develop at an ever increasing pace, the economic and social future of any country is increasingly tied to its commitment to education and training, not just for the elite but for every citizen and community.

Third, the goal is not just raising standards but changing culture. I describe this using the analogy of the driving test, a rite of passage for many young people. The emerging global information society requires us to create a new generation who, when they leave school, put on their L-plates and think 'I am a learner', rather than take them off and say 'I have passed'.

We can only make this happen on the scale needed if we value and invest in our teachers as lifelong learners themselves, not just in their 'subject skills'. To do this we need to marry the big picture of a transformed experience of learning to ICT practice, but also to new theories of learning such as learning styles or multiple intelligences. For teachers to be seen as learners themselves we need to build bridges between different areas of research – in education, learning theories, ICT and management, to name but a few.

Reading the first few titles in this series, it is wonderful to see words like creativity, personalization and exciting being based on actual evidence, not just lofty aspiration. The rate of change of technology in the next decade will at least match the progress in the last. The materials available to enrich good teaching and learning practice will grow exponentially. None of this will have the profound change that many aspire to if we cannot build the bridge between theory and what happens in individual lessons, be they in art, maths, music, history, modern languages or any other area of the curriculum.

The notion of ICT as a tool across the curriculum was greeted sceptically a decade ago. Many professionals told me that ICT may be important in maths or science, but irrelevant in the arts and humanities. My own experience is that the most exciting innovations have actually been in arts and humanities, while the notion of maths as a visual discipline seemed alien a few years ago. It has not been ICT but innovative teachers, researchers and indeed publishers who have pushed the art of the possible.

In a lot of my work, I have encouraged the notion that we should see the era we live in as a New Renaissance, rather than a new Industrial Revolution. While the industrial revolutions were about simplification and analysis, the era we live in is about synthesis and connection. We need our learners to embrace both depth and breadth to meet their needs to learn for life and living.

To the authors of this series, I offer my congratulations and sincere thanks. In bringing together the evidence of what works, the digital resources available and the new theories of learning, along with the new capabilities of ICT, they bring the focus onto the most important element of the transformation of learning, which to me is the learning needs of the teaching profession.

To the readers of this series, I make what I believe is my boldest claim. This is the greatest time in human history to be a teacher. Our societies and economies demand education like never before. Our increasing knowledge of how we learn and how the brain works, together with the availability of powerful ICT tools, make this a time when the creativity, professionalism and aspirations for a learning society are at a premium. Teaching is a noble profession. It is after all the profession that creates all the others.

There are many things that we do not yet know, so much to learn. That is what makes this so exciting. I and my colleagues at Microsoft can build the tools, but we believe that it is putting those tools in the hands of innovative, skilled and inspirational teachers that creates the real value.

I hope that after reading any of the books in this series you will feel the excitement that will make learning come alive both for you and the children you teach.

Best wishes.

Chris Yapp
Head of Public Sector Innovation
Microsoft Ltd

Author's acknowledgements

Over 25 years ago a young history teacher, Margaret Hathaway, introduced me to a simple computer database and showed me that the technology can be powerful when the educational purpose is strong. Working with rudimentary but promising software called Quest from the Advisory Unit in Hertfordshire and a set of data from the terrible Felling Colliery disaster of 1812, she demonstrated how students could search records, see connections and learn in a vivid, active way. She started me on a journey that this book seeks to continue – how we make the best of the tools of our time in the classroom.

I am thankful to many others since then who have reminded me of the role of ICT in education as being one of 'as well as' rather than 'instead of' and that the older tools of instruction that we know and love still have a use alongside newer devices. To Geoff Grounds, ex-headteacher of Sharnbrook School, I also acknowledge a debt as with his school TV assembly broadcast into every classroom (long before broadband was invented) he showed me how to match the appropriate tools to the learning need and how age shouldn't dim the passion for new opportunities which the technology might at times allow.

I would like to acknowledge the help and encouragement provided by Mike Bostock, knowing that there is indeed gold buried at the point where ICT meets learning and for helping me to clarify and connect some of the 'free range' ideas I had gathered in this field. Barbara Prashnig also deserves a special mention for her guidance and for pointing our 'educational compass' towards the potential of learning styles. Thanks to Eliza Mountford at WordRoutes for encouragement, relentless enthusiasm and early editorial help. Thanks also to Sarah Nunn for support, clarity and patient email clarifications from mainland Europe – strangely reminiscent of early radio broadcasts.

Thanks are also due to all to the schools and teachers I have worked with in the last five years especially in Redbridge in London and the Northern Grid projects in the North East of the UK. A special recognition must be given to David Ware of Little Heath School for showing how given the right tools, support and encouragement children with a variety of learning challenges can, without exaggeration, produce work which in terms of narrative power outstrips that of the BBC. Maybe Shakespeare was wrong and it's talk rather than sleep which knits up the ravelled sleeve of care. When you don't understand, a chance to check it out with your neighbour can make all the difference. I wish to acknowledge the bravery of many teachers (the silence fighters) prepared to foster talk and dialogue around the technology.

As we will see in Chapter 3 making things and telling stories takes us as far as we need to go in most learning opportunities – I commend this book to you as another step on the journey of how we might integrate the new tools of learning alongside the fundamental humanizing and extending aims of education. This book provides pointers as to how to bring the powerful alongside the precious.

As the son of a carpenter I saw from my father an early model of appropriate tool use – 'Sometimes the hammer – sometimes the plane, sometimes the chisel and work with the grain.' Finally, of course, I also saw the value of making things and sharing them with others – thanks Dad.

Chapter 1

Finding our digital longitude

▌A blueprint for ICT as it stops being a subject and becomes a transformational tool for learning

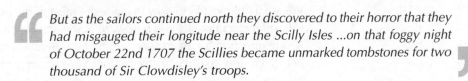

> *But as the sailors continued north they discovered to their horror that they had misgauged their longitude near the Scilly Isles ...on that foggy night of October 22nd 1707 the Scillies became unmarked tombstones for two thousand of Sir Clowdisley's troops.*

Dava Sobel (1995)

Let's call it the Moses effect – that's what we are suffering from at present – it's where you get to see the Promised Land but you don't actually get to go there. From southern Malaysia's information corridor to the virtual schools of Silicon Valley in the USA and from Finland to Soweto, we are learning slowly and painfully that information technology investment to the power of ten doesn't guarantee learning. There is something of great promise in the educational deployment of IT (or ICT as it is called in the UK) but we can't quite isolate the vital ingredients.

Yet most education systems in the world (rich and poor) have rushed to embrace ICT in the form of computers and internet connection and make it part of the curriculum. Few have thought sufficiently how it will fit and how it will help students to learn and understand. The engine driving the development is the fact (or the fear) that everybody else is doing it. We hope that our collective learning curves will be shorter in the information age but we are in danger of having too much communication and too little understanding. This book examines the role of ICT and learning in the year 2005 and suggests ways in which we can make the most of these new opportunities.

We must learn from our recent history and make some brave decisions on our future paths if we are to utilize new opportunities to meet our individual and global learning needs. It is also a time to remember the mythical characteristics of Janus, credited with the ability to look both ways – we can only move forward with new tools in learning if we remember to bring with us the lessons learned from the past. To this end our story concerns the slate, the blackboard and the television as much as it does the computer and the internet. Information and communication technology had struck when the first politician had their picture taken in front of a computer rather than a bookshelf. It's a good time to be an ICT adviser and a bad time to be a librarian – not the best way to make the most of learning opportunities for all learners.

Or if you prefer historic metaphors, there is a ship far out at sea – it knows it's a long way out but it's lost. Longitude, that second fix on position, is still 60 years from discovery. Without it no captain can know with certainty the position of his craft and many ships will flounder and sink until a timepiece is built that will work accurately at sea. In one sense, we live in similar times – technology allows learners to cover great distance at a single mouse click – we can copy and paste with ease and send messages around the globe – but often we are not sure where we are or what to do with what we have found. Even more importantly, we have no clear idea of where we are going, what we might achieve and how learning can be reignited throughout life by the creative deployment of these media rich tools in the classroom, home and workplace. We are missing a key reference point – a way of marking out the new territory so that we may occupy or move through it with purpose and clarity. Perhaps learning styles and accelerated learning techniques may well prove the longitude we seek to fix educational technology accurately in its place as learning catalyst.

We are a little lost as to how to make the most of the new tools we have. Worse still, many technocrats and hardware manufacturers would have us look in the wrong direction for an answer. For the imminent learning revolution will come not from any particular technology but from a blend of new learning approaches informed by brain research, developments in learning style analysis and findings in clinical psychology. In the next ten years, we will learn with increasing certainty how to make learning stick. I believe ICT will be a profound tool within these developments only if we rethink its use in schools.

The use of ICT in all its forms will have a dramatic and catalytic role to play in the learning revolution, especially as we learn more about subtle interplay between hearing, seeing and doing in the learning process. Yet for the moment we are in real danger of confusing the catalyst with the effect and while our gaze remains fixed on the technology, the dramatic learning opportunities it might assist may well pass us by. It's time to stop enshrining and elevating the technology and focus on the learning. In five years' time we will consider our current practice of creating computer rooms as bizarre as if the Victorians had created a specialist shrine for the use of the slate.

This is also a time of too much individual cleverness and too many 'foolish' organizations – the challenge is to ensure schools are more than 12 months smart, that is the learning and achievement of one year is available as a reference and an inspiration in subsequent years. It is a time of illusory technical promise and insufficient focus on the true fulcrums for learning. Our perceptions for the deployment of technology as an aid to learning are still too computer centric. We ignore the potential of overhead projectors, fax machines and telephones in a headlong dash to provide multiple connected computers and interactive whiteboards. We must continue to put environment first, technology second. For a poor environment with computers is still a poor environment for learning.

Just because something is desirable it doesn't mean it will happen. Individual learners, teachers and parents want to share and annotate good practice but the 'combination time bomb' of inertia, fear and overload usually intervene and prevent it. To further restrict the spread of good practice, we have, for many years, persisted with an inspection mechanism in schools which has been judgemental and debilitating and doesn't allow for the only outcome which would justify the process – the tangible sharing and celebrating of good practice. The law of information proximity informs us that what we share locally is often more valuable and less diverting than that which exists elsewhere. The age of the shared folder and the intranet is dawning and all schools should have the right and the time to develop their vocabulary of expectation as to what they want their local information sharing and celebrating to look like in electronic terms. Ten, 20 and even 30 years ago every school in the land produced a school magazine on the Banda Spirit duplicator or the photocopier. Many adults hold fond memories of the time their writing, their picture or their artwork appeared in the publication. Now it seems that fewer schools manage to produce the simplest such magazine – too much technology, too little communication. The modern day equivalent is often a website labelled 'under construction'.

Of course, this is not the whole story. Some schools are pioneering new ways of sharing the learning recipe within and beyond the school building and the school day. The challenge now is for us all to share the things that work – to tap into the bigger philanthropic brain that the internet can be – for us all to get smarter – from Soweto to Shropshire – at using these new tools.

The Banda Spirit duplicator – a key early educational technology

WITH THIS SIMPLE DEVICE STORIES WERE BROADCAST, EXPERIENCES SHARED AND STUDENT WORK REACHED AN AUDIENCE

Switch on delight

We also live at a wonderfully challenging time. We invent tools of great potential that promise much delight. Many individual teachers and learners are providing breakthrough combinations of learning approaches, achieving a synergy between what works for learners and what reinforcement and enrichment the creative use of new technology can provide. There is also a strong whiff of missed opportunity in the air. Here in the early twenty-first century as we look towards revolutions in the development of learning opportunities, we see more pointless record keeping and less creativity. Instead of deciding how new tools can make learning more delightful, teachers are overburdened with the negative undertow of excessive administration, testing and inspection. The ships of learning enlightenment lay beached on the shore of 'otherwise engaged'.

Gordon Wells (1981) says learning is the 'guided reinvention of knowledge'. To find our digital longitude we need not one single breakthrough but to foster the creative human spark of creativity and build around it. In the past, the development of ICT in schools was often driven by the technocrats – those who perceive an intrinsic value and potential within the technology to make a difference for learners. The second phase of development is now starting to yield translators, visionary individuals – those who can see the power of technology and start to map it to the needs of the subject and the learning. For every powerful application of a new tool in learning, we must search out the human dimension for that is what makes it tick and guarantees its persistence. Behind every new technological breakthough – *cherchez* the human being. Each successful deployment of ICT in our schools hinges around a human mediation and intervention. From the speaking word processors to multimedia creations, little occurs to make a difference without human intervention. For all of us the ultimate learning resource is another human being and they, as yet, do not come with plugs attached.

No matter where they are in the world, schools that can build on the firmament of learning first and technology as catalyst may well inherit the future. Schools that understand that learning is frequently the consequence of the inspiration provided by another person, and that learning can be expressed powerfully through the use of modern media, are schools equipped to keep a balanced perspective on the adoption and integration of learning technologies.

For too long ICT has been the preserve of computer advisers and computer companies with large totemic-size stands at yearly glut-spending extravaganzas like the BETT exhibition in the UK. Even government advisers with successful media backgrounds are not best placed to advise on the subtle interplay which must be invented afresh in each classroom as multimedia learning opportunities grow beyond the notional and into the mainstream.

Modern classrooms are still essentially constructed using a blueprint from Victorian times. But which group of people are best placed to design the classrooms of tomorrow? Much has been learned over recent times about the impact of environment upon learning and there is still more to learn. The choice of how space is used, movement, storage and natural light can each avoid problems commonly experienced even in quite recently constructed school buildings. The environment must reflect our developing understanding of how people best learn and how that learning is best organized. For teachers, the classroom of the future is the one they will teach in tomorrow. For learners, their life chances will be influenced by where and how they learn. Both deserve a say in the design of the classroom of the future.

Finding our longitude is about valuing and sharing individual creativity, and the local 'philanthropic will' to make things better for others.

In recent times in the UK, the need for supporting teachers to make use of the considerable bank of ICT resources placed in schools was expressed through a mass training scheme (the New Opportunities Fund ICT training scheme – a £230 million venture). Teachers would repeat lessons designed by other practitioners in order to get a certificate. This scheme aimed to put the ideas of the few into the heads of the many, when what was needed was precisely the reverse. Each of us needs to find our own point of access with the learning potential of these new tools.

At times, new tools may be the creation of a school radio station (see Chapter 3). For others, it will be the creation of a text messaging service for parents on children's weekly progress. If both these pathways are documented, annotated and shared then others will follow and improve the provision – the whole group has the potential to get smarter.

Online sharing of ideas in small groups is one of the most profound contributions so far to make things better and more manageable for teachers. Remember our right to be different – homogenization only really works for milk.

One of the most important things is to use tools to help students and teachers make something to ensure the diet of ICT goes beyond copy, paste and adapt. We will look at ideas from flicker books and plasticine Shakespeare to schools running their own radio stations (see Chapters 3 and 4). At times, our skills focus too heavily in proscribed curricular for the teaching of something which is a tool not a subject; however, this will change for the creative use of ICT is now planted and growing naturally within subject areas. Technologies of the classroom will continue to flex and change faster than we can categorize them. ICT won't stay still long enough to have a subject built around it – so let's wise up to the fact that we are dealing with a profound set of tools.

To see the interconnectedness of knowledge, the cross-curricular objectives of many past curriculum designers are no longer an aspiration but an inevitability. Learners around the world cannot but benefit as long as we get it right.

One of the key maxims for accelerated learning is to create an environment with high challenge and low threat. This concept should serve to underpin the design and deployment of ICT tasks in schools. Too much use of ICT for the 'sake of it', for example, using clip art and wizards, can take children away from the creative surge and into the doldrums of low challenge and even lower expectation. Witness much of the 'keeping them quiet work' which has come to blight the early use of ICT in schools. Without creativity, the much-heralded motivation that students display when using ICT will be short lived; as home access to technology grows, school use without the key ingredient of creativity will become jaded. The simplest way to provide this is to get the students making things and sharing them with a local audience over existing, already established school networks.

Similarly, schools leading the field must take up the challenge of continued development and innovation with new learning opportunities in mind. This involves the environment, the tool sets and activities of instruction. Restaurants look at work flow and environment design and development at six monthly intervals – schools do the same only once each generation, or so it seems.

So we look to the deployment of new tools in a very old dispensation called school. We will be wise to expect some tectonic tension as the plates move once more and also to witness some unbelievable opportunities to change things for the better that must be seized before they pass us by.

It's time for us all 'to find our own religion' and point of access for new tools as we are moving beyond blind faith towards a productive journey where teachers with their own space, time and tools will find their own point of access.

The fulcrums of learning

To move forward, we must not celebrate the technology but welcome the opportunity to work more productively with a variety of learning strengths and needs for learners of all abilities, and families of every social status.

New tools must also be deployed to encourage purposeful talk about what is being learned. Make no mistake – no matter how hard we avoid it because it is difficult to measure – the fulcrums for learning are the mouth and ears. In addition, we have the opportunity to make learning social, with the help of tools like classroom data projectors, for if there is a world of information out there it shouldn't be constrained within a 13-inch window. Sound – the poor relation because in the past it's been hard to manage and mark – is also set to come centre stage. In reality, all ICT has given us so far is dumb text on screen for the last 20 years. The rise of the MP3 sound file, perfectly fit for purpose in carrying good quality sound across the wire, may change that forever. Put another way, many schools have hundred thousand pound networks running Office software in silence. Why? Schools are not offices? Our paradigm for the use of ICT in schools is one built on the office, which was in turn built on the typing pool – a simple manufactory of words. It no longer fits or suits our needs and it's time we looked elsewhere for our models of technology integration.

Who pays and who learns?

Many poorer families will have no direct access to the tools of email and internet access. Financial exclusion is serious, yet conceptual exclusion is much more pernicious – precious moments of exploration and creative use of new tools are more likely to happen, like the seeds of reading, in the home or the social group, rather than in school.

In one sense, we are behind the Victorians in their commitment to universal access. Their creation of lending libraries and learning co-operatives displayed a more practical grasp about building from the core concept of universal access ideas into physical structures that changed lives. Places where all could apply for membership and find a book tied into the aspirations of even the poorest; and more importantly, it was culturally acceptable to be part of the movement. Local libraries and City Learning Centres are starting to provide alternative places for internet access.

Companies with little pedagogic knowledge and no altruistic intent are currently attempting to drive the technological revolution in learning or at least standing between schools and communities in their attempt to drive this revolution forwards.

Let's look at the historical backdrop to our times. Our gaze might fall on the reflected wisdoms of 10,000 years of technological development and across many cultures. At each point of focus we would see dramatic examples of the visual arts, music and emergent science. Often this learning was underpinned and memorized in the oral tradition and extended by the weaving of a narrative skein that kept it together and allowed it to be passed on.

We are starting to see with increasing clarity that these ancient and successful methods worked in part by providing a fast track path to long-term memory by pole-bridging between different parts of the brain and by accessing the subconscious mind. Deep within the brains of our ancestors connections were made. By evoking an emotional response to words, pictures, music and rhythm their brains focused, paid attention, and the roots of memory started to grow.

Multisensory learning environments are not as new as we might think

For many learners, the past wisdoms of true multimedia learning have been forgotten in learning approaches that are too often silent, and dependent on text alone to convey meaning. New understanding and new tools will give us the opportunity to adjust the diet according to need. It is time to look afresh at the variety of tools available and for schools to decide where ICT fits in with their agenda as a tool for teachers and learners. Lozanov, the developer of the first accelerated learning approaches, discovered the unique way in which sound may alter mood and assist learning and we now have the option to ally sound and image more purposefully in the classroom.

 Stop implementing technology in our schools – it doesn't work, instead let's redefine literacy and implement that.

David Warlick (2004)

Visualization, the personal and internal mind's eye masterpiece that each of us presents as our own private show, is not replicable by anything screen generated. Now imagine walking through the doors and into the school of the future – some bubbly Bach plays on the school surround sound system and today's learning menu floats holographically in the middle distance as your mentor walks towards you with a greeting. For the ultimate learning resource is another person – technology will not change this but it will help to make human resources available over distance and time. The rest of this book concerns practical ways in which we can move forward and find our personal longitude where accelerated learning meets ICT in an increasingly digital world.

Chapter 2

New learning opportunities

 Any sufficiently advanced technology is indistinguishable from magic.

Arthur C. Clarke (1999)

'May you live in interesting times' goes the old Chinese curse and it's clear that we do. We can also turn this into a blessing however. For the opportunity now exists to combine our emergent knowledge about the brain and learning with the power of educational technology tools, and use this synergy to provide new learning opportunities in the classroom, the library and the home.

To make the most of this opportunity, we need to combine the knowledge of how learning happens most effectively with the emergent power of ICT. ICT is potentially both an amplifier and a catalyst par excellence in the learning process. As we follow these paths, we may find that we will stop treating ICT as a subject and instead consider its role as a profound learning tool and medium of exchange and connection.

▌ Synergy at gathering pace

 But I know a change is gonna come
Oh, yes it will, look it here,

'A change is gonna come', Al Green

For many in the connected world, teaching and learning will never be the same again – new models will emerge shaped by the application of new tools, individual schools, learners and teachers. It's time to investigate and unlock ICT's potential as a tool to help us learn and as a medium for communication.

Riding the wave of change – learning technologies meet learning theory

transformational change

The development of the printing press was a key technological and cultural event replacing the oral tradition with printed finality and elevating the position of the written word to that of key carrier medium for learning and knowledge. With the laptop, mobile phone and the internet, the coming developments are more likely to resemble transformational change – when it passes and we look afresh at the topography of the classroom it will have changed forever.

 Technological change is not additive; it is ecological. I can explain this best by an analogy. What happens if we place a drop of red dye into a beaker of clear water? Do we have clear water plus a spot of red dye? Obviously not. We have a new coloration to every molecule of water... In the year 1500, after the printing press was invented, you did not have old Europe plus the printing press. You had a different Europe.

N. Postman (1992)

▊ Many paths to the future

The best way to consider the use of new technology in the learning process is as a range of tools, deployed when appropriate and when the teacher, student or school feels confident in their use. Our focus should be on the opportunities provided by this range of tools rather than on one particular technology however beguiling or prevalent it might be at any particular time. At times, a school may need an interactive whiteboard, at other times a projector and air mouse may fit the bill and set the teacher free from the front of the class, while providing a low cost device to pass around for students to take control. At other times, pencil and paper may be more suitable. Appropriate technology rules OK.

Historical experience has taught us to avoid second-guessing the future path and application of technology in the learning process. In four years the mobile phone has gone from a banned item in schools to a learning and assessment device. Meantime the 'school computer suite' has begun a similar (but reversed) journey into oblivion. We should not be surprised by these developments – in fact we should continue to expect such surprises in the future and make this 'apparent uncertainty' part of our planning.

Teachers have always aimed to include a range of resources and activities in their classroom work so that they can teach in different ways and for students to learn with some choice and variety. No single technology should subvert the inclinations and aptitudes of the teacher or the school. For the school vision and the personal aptitude and preference of the individual teacher is the key influence on the adoption and sustainability of any ICT development. On paper and the computer, some of these resources hold the promise for self-instruction and second-chance learning beyond the classroom. For too long, technology has ensured that schools do things the same – it's time now to allow them to be different. For we shall see a trust yourself time; dare to be different and deploy the tools as they meet your needs and suit your style.

Shared understanding of opportunities at school level also leads to the end of individual cleverness, which has plagued much of the early promise of ICT in schools, where others seek to impress you with their prowess rather than take you forward in your own understanding. Sharing the learning recipe can be greatly assisted through simple but systemic ICT developments like the establishment of a 'shared area' on the school computer network, where resources and exemplars of work may be published and where magically they will remain even when 'taken away' by others – a new digital riddle of our times.

Sometimes simple 'intermediate technology' interventions have more to recommend them than large-scale investment, in particular, computer provision. Consider the slate, now back in classrooms once more, as small white plastic whiteboards. These small squares of plastic allow students to explore the provisionality of the written word – to 'have a go' at spelling or calculation knowing they can wipe it out and start again. Such resources help provide high challenge and low threat – the undo command existed on slates 10,000 years or so before the digital equivalent was invented. Teachers have devised a myriad of uses for these simple tools, from sharing notes, to whole-class feedback on how confident students feel about some new learning they have done.

The slate rides again – if you want a good idea for the future, have a glance at the past

The age of e-learning calls for a time when learners will have access to learning tools, resources and support beyond the traditional confines of the classroom and the lecture theatre. It is, ICT suppliers tell us, the age of Martini (anytime – anywhere) learning and schools are invited to think about 24/7 (twenty four hours a day, seven days a week). Access to learning resources via internet connection bring to life the idea of a school that never closes in terms of access to learning resources and other learners, albeit at a geographical distance. The reality for most is far removed from such scenarios at present but some of what it foretells will come to pass – it is a responsibility and opportunity for all of us to shape the development and deployments so that learning benefits, becomes more delightful and the technology is kept in its place as a tool.

In search of the ultimate learning resource

The good news is that the ultimate learning resource does not have a plug attached. It is another person helping you, especially in the moments when your cognitive penny fails to drop. Sometimes this person will be cognitively remote, sometimes they will be physically at a distance. Unless digital learning opportunities are mediated by a mentor/teacher/significant other their effect and potential are limited.

The ultimate learning resource

the technician

the teacher

a student

the ulr is another person

The technician who makes the equipment 'sing'. The teacher arriving at your desk just at the moment that your 'cognitive penny fails to drop'. The student sitting next to you who explains something simply.

The use of new tools will also reveal new ways of doing things, which make a difference to the range, depth and method of learning. Ideally this will help, or force, us to challenge misconceptions. Like water finding its own level, learners eventually find a way to learn. Ours is both the opportunity and the responsibility, as Bruner notes, of the mantle that passes to each new age of teachers and learners.

 I shall take it as self evident that each generation must define afresh the nature, direction and aims of education to assure such freedom and rationality as can be attained for a future generation.

J. Bruner (1966)

Accelerated learning meets ICT
Accelerated learning is a generic term to describe a set of classroom strategies and skills that help students learn more effectively. Some of the central tenets are:

➡ Stress kills (or severely reduces) learning opportunities
➡ Students need to see, hear and feel the big picture
➡ We need to connect learning to make it memorable
➡ Music can change learning environments for the better; and increase students' predisposition to learn
➡ We each learn in a unique variety of ways through our senses.

As if by magic, just as our knowledge and understanding of the brain and learning theory is developing, we now have new classroom tools to help us support many of its key principles. Data projectors linked to computers can fill a classroom wall with a still or moving image and provide new opportunities for showing the big picture at the start of a lesson, using image as a part of the teaching process and for rolling a scrolling review of what has been learned at the end. Interactive whiteboards at times provide teachers and students with a kinesthetic and tactile teaching and learning opportunity.

Sound and video, previously two linear formats, may now be recorded, edited and accessed for replay with digital accuracy on the computer. Learning resources stored online allow access outside class and second chance learning opportunities. Similarly, computer software, with features like the 'undo command', at times provide the ideal tool to make the learning high challenge but low threat. The computer (arch organizer) can also allow teachers to play an appropriate music file to begin a lesson, to energize or accompany a review at a single mouse click. In this chapter, we will explore how to make the most of this coming together, this digital synergy for learning.

The timing of these parallel developments is of major significance for those involved in education in all sectors and phases. Our knowledge and understanding of learning and how it happens is developing rapidly just at the point where we are exploring new classroom tools to help us support many of its key requirements.

Using ICT in the accelerated learning process
ICT can help to:

➡ Lower threat and can provide second and third chance learning.

➡ Provide different points of access for learners with different learning styles.

➡ Allow teachers to create, store and deploy multimedia resources and activities to work with different visual, auditory and kinesthetic modalities.

➡ Provide new ways of making connections – allows student to present their understanding in a media over which they have some mastery, for example, a sound file, a scanned picture, animation and hypertext – a tool to make connections and say 'this links with that'.

➡ Provide support and scaffolding, safe within the cradle of the 'undo command', giving opportunities for second and third chance learning without the fear of failure or the stress of others seeing that 'you haven't got it yet'.

We break free of the linear when we jump around in speech, it's harder to do this in text, although writers such as Lawrence Sterne and James Joyce, among others, have had a good go. We make connections by linking one idea with another and use ICT when we use the tool of hypertext to link one word, sound or image with another.

Just as we become secure in our understanding that learning is about seeing connections – technology has provided a suitable echo, a metaphor and a tool for making connections in the form of new tools and specific resources such as hypertext.

The better connected the two halves of the brain, the greater the potential of the brain for learning and creativity.

Colin Rose (1992)

Learning is about seeing connections. The opportunity to move around an area of subject knowledge and forge connections, sometimes with the aid of ICT, allows learners to develop a key understanding of the range of a subject and see how it fits together.

It is another central tenet of accelerated learning that there are no limits to the brain's capacity to learn. It's also true that this can be extended and scaffolded by the use of ICT where learners take chances, safe within the cradle of the 'undo command'. The challenge for teachers is to focus on the stress reducing capability of ICT as well as upping the challenge in terms of tools used and activities set.

Creatively deployed, ICT may prove a 'trojan mouse' resource – smuggling fun and creativity back into the curriculum, lowering threat but allowing students to take risks and learn by doing and making things. To make the greatest difference, however, ICT should be used as an integral part of teaching and learning developments within schools. At times, the slingshot effect that ICT can help provide allows students to drop 'into the flow' and escape the gravitational pull of inertial and low motivation. ICT has the cachet of a learning conduit that is perceived as street cool and as such can be utilized to the maximum extent. From touchstone to amplifier, let's now investigate the slingshot effect in action.

 Too often, it has been assumed that ICT will transform learning. It won't if it is being incorporated into a traditional teaching structure but its effects are maximized if it goes hand in hand with changes in teaching and learning.

Derek Wise, headteacher, Cramlington Community High School

How we learn and how we might intervene to 'help the process along' is a subject that has fascinated mankind for millennia. Most early writers noted the subtle interplay between understanding and interaction – learning is at some level about 'doing'. For many of us the more visceral the doing, the better we learn. The word education has its roots in the Latin 'educere', meaning to 'draw out – to lead'. Gordon Wells writing a few thousand years later was still focused on learning being the 'guided reinvention of knowledge'.

Consider for a moment the human brain with 100 billion neurons.

Across the synapse, down the line, says the hand to the brain, 'I'm doing fine'

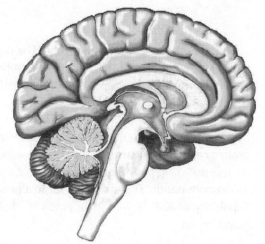

Remember the human brain is an analogue, constantly varying, chemical soup of a communications centre – forever making, forging, remembering and losing connections rather than a device of digital fixity: 100 billion neurons each with axons and dendrites with synaptic gaps across which chemical communication flows.

In the last ten years, increased knowledge of the brain and the ability to measure discrete brain activity during learning activities has allowed us to look more closely at what happens when we learn. We have started to map different ways in which we might describe the range and nature of intelligence. We also see direct evidence of how repeated learning experiences can change the very physical structure of the brain.

The 'use it or lose it' maxim anticipates the forging of connection necessary for learning to take place and the high challenge and low threat present in well designed and supported learning opportunities. Professor Phil Race (1996) notes that learning starts with wanting, which in turn leads into the doing as the process emanates outwards like a ripple on a pond.

Getting the learning environment right

It's clear that for many learners the computer exerts a motivational pull. At times, with appropriate use, it can scaffold the learner, encourage bravery and some risk taking and allow fast interactive learning from mistakes which can then be undone and retraced. In one sense the new tools represent a prize or a gift that we must not dissipate. So we should resist the temptation to use the computer as a digital childminder – a tool to keep them quiet on a diet of word processing and 'cut and paste' ease.

Many teachers encourage students to celebrate the moment when they are 'stuck' as they are about to do some key learning. Into such a climate, the seed of formative assessment should be planted. In the primary class of Bailey's Court School in Bristol a poster says 'You're stuck? Good! Now you are ready to do some serious learning.'

 Create an environment where errors are made explicit and accepted as a necessary part in moving towards understanding.

Professor Chris Harrison (2004)

One of our core abilities as a species is to learn almost without helping it, when the conditions are right and the brain responds to challenge. Unfortunately the capacity to learn also closes down under threat.

Stress kills learning opportunities

How to reduce stress but keep the challenge high is the conundrum for teachers as they plan learning activities. Too much early use of ICT has led to low challenge, low threat 'cut and paste' ease and now it's time to up the stakes. The parallel challenge is in designing activities to help students 'come to know' in the way that is most vivid, tuneful and graphic for them – where the tools are the props, and activities are the pathways in the learning experience.

Comenius writing in 1649 could be considered the grandfather of accelerated learning. He stated that 'all learners were born with a natural craving for knowledge' (until schools beat it out of them he implied) and he affirmed the need to learn through experience in stress reducing 'easy stages'. His appeal to full sensory learning is an eloquent rebuttal of talk and text as the dominant pedagogy pathway of past times.

> *If possible, let everything be perceived by all senses, things seen by the eyes, things heard by the ears, things smelt by the nose as well as things tasted by the tongue. If possible let something be perceived by all senses together, let it happen. There is nothing in wisdom, which hasn't been perceived by senses. So, why should learning not start by material presentation rather than by oral explanation?*

J.A. Comenius (1649)

Less is sometimes more

There is also the danger that we will miss the opportunity provided by the subtle and the simple in our rush to integrate the latest technology in schools. So it's important to note that many of the key principles of accelerated learning can be assisted with simple and rudimentary props like a tape player and wall posters. We have also come to realize that latest isn't always the best – that older tools still have a place to play and the design of the task and quality of interaction matters most. Sometimes with ICT, less is more.

In South Africa's Cape Province, a mass literacy scheme entitled 'English in Action' (an accelerated learning programme) is built around simple radio broadcasts and posters sent to schools in advance, which are then used interactively as part of the programme. The children look forward to the programme and the teachers enjoy professional development – as the radio broadcast talks directly to the staff at times explaining why they are carrying out each exercise. From just three colourful posters and a weekly radio broadcast, the programme has achieved massive success and coverage and improvement in retention and teacher confidence, as well as a way of introducing new pedagogy and practice. If we were to write a sensory recipe for this learning opportunity we would note that students had a complete VAK experience as dance and song accompanied the listening and the speaking, especially if they were called to the front to demonstrate and act out part of the lesson for others. Perhaps the UK's national literacy/numeracy strategy could learn from this model. We could ease the numeracy burden on many teachers by supplying good visual and interactive resources to schools and by using a daily internet based radio programme to guide teachers in their use.

If we have access to computers and an internet connection, ICT brings new opportunities to access external resources and to make access to sound and image easier to manage. It can also increase the opportunities in practice for teachers to integrate these media tools into their daily classroom teaching.

The central principles of accelerated learning have led to the development of practical implementation strategies for the classroom in the shape of a cyclical structure or a recipe – these Accelerated Learning Cycles are now in use by many teachers.

New tools make a difference

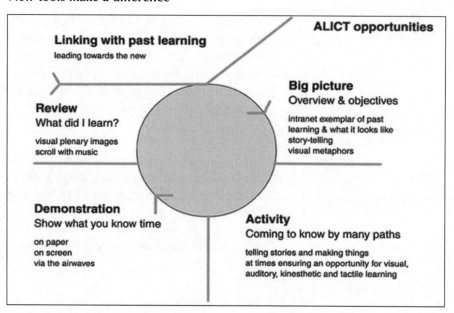

In some of these areas of classroom management and integration of accelerated learning, ICT has a unique contribution to make – sometimes as a management tool to make sure that the right music plays when the mouse is clicked and sometimes as the engine to connect the learning graphically in a mind map with sound and image alongside text or to manage a visual plenary with image, sound and movement serving to make a review memorable and provide more than one point of access. Finally through publishing locally students have the opportunity to revisit, replay and more than one chance to understand.

All learners are different

We all learn in a range of different ways – each one of us has a number of preferred ways of learning. Yet for us all, whatever our preferred motivations and method of input, learning is ultimately a process of seeing, holding onto and recalling connections. We know from research and from our intuitive experience as teachers and learners that as far as learning is concerned, one size doesn't fit all.

One way of characterizing the different needs of learners is to focus on the ways in which they might best receive instruction – especially when they are 'stuck' or the task is new and challenging. Through what combination of sensory input, environmental factors and activities are the conditions for learning made optimum for individual learners? The 'tectonic plates', which characterized the current fixity of our continents of pedagogy and knowledge of cognition, are once more on the move.

Paradoxically the best that we might do with this knowledge is not to start down the road of the personalized curriculum that might be philosophically and culturally unattainable, but to look for the broad commonality of needs and deploy our repertoires of instruction around them. Best in fact to be aware of difference but plan for the broad style and sensory commonalities in learning styles and needs. Finally we must take the opportunity of our times and use ICT tools to broaden the sensory bandwidth of instruction providing support for the range of learning modalities.

For just as our knowledge of learning style needs and preferences increases, and our diagnoses of individual learning style profiles becomes more precise, technology has expanded our classroom toolkit for teaching and given us tools to work with our learners' strengths. We are learning more about the fragile interplay between visual, auditory, tactile and kinesthetic learning needs just at the time that our new classroom tools give us the ability to support and foster these modalities in the classroom.

We are also learning more about student learning styles and the conditions under which they are likely to learn most effectively. Work from Dunn (2000) and Howard Gardner (1983), among others, has allowed diagnostic broad-brush tools to be developed that suggest key considerations for learning preference profiles for all learners. Whatever limitations individual profiles may have, their contribution in developing the focus on difference and the limitless potential in individual learners is substantive. If we accept the premise that not everyone learns in the same way, then learning styles give us a diagnostic tool to focus on range and difference among learners. ICT then provides us with some resources so that we can work with a range of different learning style needs in the classroom.

The opportunity now is to focus on not what is possible but what is powerful in connecting the learning, engaging the senses and getting the learning across. We remember things we feel strongly about whether in visual or auditory formats – stories in particular are something we can't resist responding to. The spoken word, and images (especially when linked to music) are all powerful ways teachers can utilize a range of low-tech resources in their classroom to maximum effect. As we will see, story-telling is back with some digital amplification and certainty.

The sum is greater than the parts

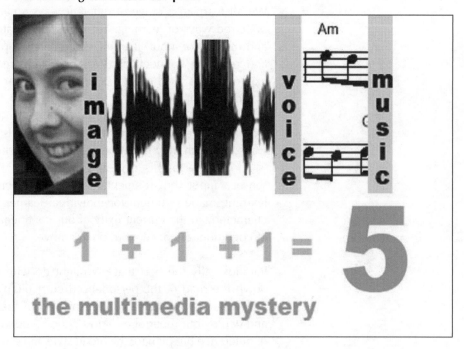

There are a range of providers of individual learning style profiles: each use a slightly different method of classification with the common central idea that we all have particular strengths and preferences and that these map, in some way, to our sensory modalities, the various ways we prefer to take in information through our senses of sight, hearing and touch.

Type 'learning styles questionnaire' into a search engine like Google and you are presented with over a hundred thousand matches – many of them sites where you can answer a few questions of how you like to learn before you are told what your dominant learning style features are. The procedure is surprisingly simple. The process also starts to make the learner a little more self-aware and curious about how they might learn most effectively. All current instruments to diagnose learning style are basic and imperfect but they are still useful in that they help us move the focus inexorably onto learning and what makes it work most efficiently and delightfully. They may also point the way to future career paths.

One of the key requirements for a successful learning experience is for both teacher and learner to be aware of the variety of styles present within a learning group. Learners can 'come to understand' by many pathways but listen, read and write are by far the most popular tracks used in schools leading neatly into an exam system that uses the same approach. This is probably for two reasons – teachers themselves may have a preference for these modalities and it is also a very efficient way of 'delivering' the large amounts of content that many over-designed curriculums now contain.

Searching for the firm ground of certainty in the shifting fields of multiple intelligence and learning styles is difficult. Perhaps the most sensible approach is to imagine that every child should arrive at a point at some time in their school career and lifetime as conductor of their own learning – where they get to organize and interpret the different instruments of instruction and become composers of their own understanding.

The age of 'do it yourself'

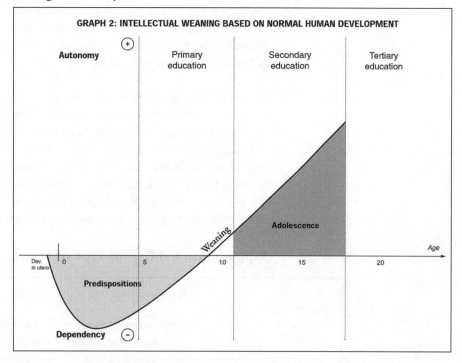

In his book, *The Unfinished Revolution*, John Abbott (2000) describes a concept called 'intellectual weaning' (see graph above), where the dependency of the learner on other people changes over time. He says, 'the more skills the learner acquires, the more the learner is responsible for using those skills. Learning therefore follows a strict weaning process.' In this model we can see that there is a biological necessity for growing autonomy for the learner at the time that young people go through their years of secondary education. Opportunities for students to be conductors of their own learning are congruent with their taking increased responsibility for their own learning.

Classroom magic supported by a range of classroom technology

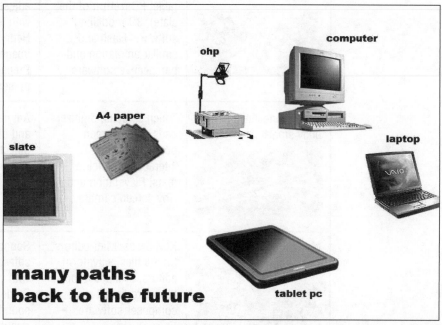

From the A4 handout to the video tape player and on to the overhead projector (OHP), the desktop computer, the laptop and new digital tablet.

In 1983, Dr Howard Gardner, professor of education at Harvard University, developed the theory of multiple intelligence. He suggested that the original idea of intelligence, based on IQ score, is far too limited. Instead, Gardner suggested eight different intelligences to account for a broader range of human potential in children and adults.

The work done by Dr Howard Gardner on multiple intelligence has led many to recognize that intelligence relates to several distinct capabilities and is not fixed in the conventional sense – that each person's blend of capability reveals a unique cognitive profile. Again, these descriptions and mappings of individual intelligence lack the refinement and precision that later research and learning theory development may yield. However, for now we must console ourselves with the fact that 'blunt instruments make good signposts' and they are clearly pointing the way to making a difference for the better for learners.

Tapping into a different type of smart

	Tools	Tasks
Linguistic: word smart	Email, speaking word processors and screen tools, sound editing software like Audacity, videoconferencing and microphones.	Talk radio show host on school internet radio, electronic text analysis, etymology research, mind map software, for example, Inspiration. Searching Google for word-parts and connections.
Logical–mathematical: number/reasoning smart	Spreadsheets, programmable calculators, web page editing, multimedia authoring software and Flash action scripting.	Design puzzles for others. Write an interactive timetable for local sharing via shared folder or intranet with others in film/animation production. Classification and hierarchy work using visual tools.
Spatial: picture smart	Scanner, graphics tablet, tablet PC (return of the slate), 3D modelling software, Flash and similar animation and perspective software.	Multi-image collage, annotation and adjustment of images. Comic design with learning content, for example, Henry and his wives. Search using images on search engines like Google. Prepare turbo-teaching visual presentations.
Bodily–kinesthetic: body smart	Touch screens, digitizer pads, large screen projection and interaction, dancing mats, Playstation and iToy screen camera.	Animation work with modelling clay and digital cameras, animating 2D objects, for example, gears, wheels, cars and animals.
Musical: music smart	Keyboards. Midi-editors. Sound files, waveform editors, broadcast tools, keyboard linked to composer software.	Soundtracks for media projects. Ejay software for loops work. Midi files with wrong notes that need fixing. Students composing their own soundtracks at around 60 beats per minute for concert review work.

	Tools	Tasks
Interpersonal: people smart	Word-processing, email, intranet and web publishing.	Interviews for radio and digital video editing, digital story-telling work. Assistance with tutorial support for other students after large group learning activities
Intrapersonal: self-smart	Word-processing/sound file recorder with MP3 output.	Diary, anonymous reflective work, assisting in running a question/answer intranet board on feelings and school life and learning opportunities.
Naturalist: nature smart	Sound recorder, still camera, portable listening devices, for example, iPod, global positioning receiver.	Multimedia field study zoom in and explain environments (classes in Finland have mobile phones given to them to keep in touch and receive further instructions for learning while they are outside school working on projects). Making your own annotated walks linked to global positioning data.

Matching the power of ICT to VAK

Forget the punishment fitting the crime, it's time to match the technology to the style. At last we have a chance to bring a little more purpose and precision to the why and how of ICT in the classroom.

Learning and learning in the widening gyre

Pick 'n' mix: seeing, listening, doing

Below we plot some of the potential uses of ICT as a support for different learning styles

Visual: I see
- Students see the big picture
- Take and manipulate images
- Edit their own short video
- Label a picture to tell a story

Auditory: I hear
- Students record their own talking stories
- Text to MP3 conversion allows text to be heard
- Students proof listen to their work on portable MP3 players

Big picture Display

Learning central
Tools are props, activities are pathways

Good quality playback

Destination learning central

Place to play, model, make and draw. It's taking the sandpit to secondary school

Learning styles ICT Audit
How VAK is your software provision in school?
How many ways do you have
- of working with text?
- of recording and editing sound?
- of cropping resizing and editing the still image?
- of working with the moving image and editing clips?
- of playing music and editing the results on the computer?

Kinesthetic: I do
- Students play keyboard and guitar and edit and enhance the track on screen
- Plasticine and models are available for making animation stories
- Tablet PC allows them to trace and draw by hand

ICT a good shepherd in the slow stages

Learning pace isn't constant – when you're stuck you learn slowly, when you're 'in the flow' you learn fast. Activities which allow learners to build and share using hand, eye and mouth are a useful way of providing the space and time needed for learners to become unstuck, see connection and think about their approach to learning. ICT is particularly suited to supporting the 'slow stages', lowering threat and allowing second chances to learn. The use of templates where a structure is provided for the learner to work within, speaking word processors which turn text to talk and similar tools all help shepherd learners through the 'stuck times'.

The use of preferred modalities is best thought of as a learning input stage with the four sensory inputs providing paths through which students can receive information. We all learn in slightly different ways but patterns emerge regarding individual preferences for learning by hearing, doing, seeing and (some would argue) touching. These style preferences are then given the grander titles of visual, auditory, kinesthetic and tactile (the touchers).

Much of the work done with individual learning styles by different researchers centres around three or four dominant modalities, of VAK and T. This model is in part derived from NLP (Neuro-Linguistic Programming) which some might characterize as an attempt to 'copyright common sense'. Early NLP researchers in the US looked at people who could do things well and then wrote the 'recipe of success' for others to follow. The process was known as modelling and it was developed as a way of working out what stages and methods of learning and gathering information people use when they learn well – then writing the recipe for others to follow. So somebody imagining taking a successful penalty kick might first hear an inner voice telling him to be calm (auditory internal), followed by a feeling of relaxation in the body and the legs (kinesthetic external), followed by a visual recollection of penalties successfully converted in the past (visual internal). The recipe for this process for others to follow could be written as: Ai > Ke > Vi = goal.

Using a series of short profile questions, general observations can be suggested about any individual learner's preferred modality for taking in new information. As with the practice of medicine through observation of symptoms, most of what these questions reveal can be observed by watching children carefully and listening to what they say. Do they find it easy to listen? Do they prefer to view and is sitting in their seat for a long time a difficult challenge? Does their language tell you that they see the answer or does it feel right to them? Do they suddenly come alive when a task allows them to work in their preferred modality – when they have to draw, record a sound or simply get sent on a message? What areas need development and what are the surest pathways through to them when the subject being taught is new and difficult?

Practical learning style audits are now carried out in an increasing number of schools in the US, Scandinavia, New Zealand and the UK. The promise of these developing diagnostics is that the fit between teaching style and learning style can at last become more than a chance event. At the very least, it will help teachers guard against the tendency for their preferred learning style to become their preferred and exclusive teaching style. Individual plans may indeed be a future possibility, but for now the potential is to be aware of the broad-brush group profiles.

No one learning style instrument is ever likely to provide the definitive answer in terms of classroom pedagogy. But we are closer to the point when we will be able to deploy approaches and resources according to learning need or at least to ensure a balance and a range in the learning diet for the diverse groups of learners who gather in front of us to be taught and to learn. Some schools are using questionnaires and audits with students to deduce their learning styles profiles, and then issue colour coded cards detailing students' dominant learning style. In some schools, these are left out on tables during lessons providing teachers with visual cues as to the number of learners with particular dominant learning preferences.

There is a danger that too much of a focus might fall on the impossible task of meeting a variety of needs. There is no such thing as an exclusively auditory or kinesthetic learner and it's counter productive to label learners in such a simplistic fashion. All learners have a unique mix of different learning needs and requirements and the use of ICT simply offers us new opportunities for meeting some of these needs. In addition, it allows students to communicate their understanding in a variety of ways, which can at times be guided by individual capability and preference. The bandwidth of instruction has been narrow and focused on a particular type of learner. However, now we can broaden this. Teachers note the immediate change in a learner or group when the type of teaching or the nature of the task allows them to work in an area of learning style preference.

None of this should serve to lessen the challenge and effort required on behalf of the learner. Professor Guy Claxton notes that learning will in some senses be a struggle if 'muscle' is to be built. One way to consider the current work on learning styles is as a lens focusing our attention on the detail of the range and diversity which learners display in their learning.

WEBSITE

What schools need now is a sense of recognition of difference and a full portfolio of models from which to derive their own philosophy and practical response. Whether these are Professor Guy Claxton's four Rs of *Resilience, Reflectiveness, Resourcefulness* and *Reciprocity* (from Futurelab presentation www.nestafuturelab.org) or Kolbe's *Experiencing, Reflecting, Concluding and Planning Cycle*, matters less than the fact we are deploying the tools of our time in a reflective fashion with learning development in mind and ICT firmly kept in place as a catalytic tool.

This is not to envisage a nightmare scenario of a teacher greeting a class with the commands, 'auditory learners over there, get your headphones on and visual dominants get your virtual reality goggles fitted', for this serves nobody well. Each learner should have the opportunity at times to learn in a way that works best for them as part of their learning experience – and at other times they should also have the opportunity to 'build the muscles' of working in an area of weakness. Even if a student's preferred style is met for just a small part of their educational experience the effects can be dramatic and positive.

The model of learning that each school must develop and adjust for themselves should include range and diversity along with precision and perseverance. The challenge is to combine the meeting of a 'style need' perhaps to bring a 'stuck' or disaffected student back into the learning fold with well designed low threat, high challenge learning activities to build the 'stamina of perseverance'.

The local and, at times, social building of knowledge in schools and their communities is one of the keys to the future even in an increasingly connected world. What follows in the book are some tools and approaches for you, the teacher, to slot into individual provision as you see fit. For the learning revolution to be successful, schools, teachers and learners must be constructors and developers of their own tools for learning.

'From Vygotsky (1962) through Papert (1980), Bruner (1975) and Wood (1988) we can see a reasonable consensus that learning is doing, and doing socially. Indeed from Plato through Locke to your grandparents this unstartling view of successful learning has had common currency. It might be described as constructivist; understanding built through conversation and critical friendship, through constructing artifacts and reflecting on them.'

Professor Stephen Heppell (2002)

We all learn in part by doing, making and being active in the learning process – tools allowing us to make the most of a variety of sensory modalities, such as hearing, seeing and touching, help at times to bring the learning to life and help make it stick. As we shall see in the next chapter the deployment of key tools and the design of learning activities are two ways in which we allow students, at least for part of their educational experience, to be active conductors of their own learning.

Chapter 3

Tools & activities to make a difference

▌Telling stories and teaching each other – five pathway projects

In the beginning there was the slate, the teacher and a monitor: nothing electrical, just an older child. We wrote by rote and copied in cursive hand. Our resources were each other, our collective experience and what the teacher told us. We wrote without audience, our teacher read it and the slate was wiped clean. Our slate lasted a hundred years or so. Books appeared with tangible words and images. We learned to search for information and our curriculum grew. It grew because new resources led to new questions and, almost without realizing it, our audience broadened. But our best resources are still each other as the technology is powerful only when the educational purpose is strong.

 I beg to leave, to hear your wondrous stories.

'Wondrous Stories', Jon Anderson

Many schools, especially primaries, are exploring the potential of building some of the curriculum around the telling and the sharing of stories. To this end, they are using a variety of story-telling tools to provide 'text-extending opportunities' so that learners can display and share their understanding in a medium over which they have some mastery. This chapter is about how schools can tell and share stories about their own learning and experiences using sound, image, animation, drawing and film.

Sometimes we learn more deeply, quickly, happily making and adapting our own material than digesting the polished work of others. This is particularly true when we can use the range of media options provided by some ICT tools, where students can be directly involved in creating quality resources as a direct part of their learning. In addition, these resources can also enjoy a second life adding to local stores of knowledge and experience and providing props for other learners.

Learning is concerned with seeing connections then holding and expanding them over time. Activities and tools which allow this construction, articulation and presentation of knowledge, provide a reinforcement and a physical external representation of what happens in our minds as we learn, make connections and remember.

Developing a learning materials production centre and whole-school approach requires:

➡ ICT in the role of production tool, stimulus and means of storing and sharing

➡ Schools in the driving seat in the process as arbiters, developers and sharers of their own stories

➡ Activities developed to produce resources which demonstrate on a regular basis and in a variety of media 'this is what learning looks like here'.

In parallel, we also have the opportunity to raise the bar in terms of challenge and expectations. Students of a young age can produce high quality resources containing a range of media especially when assisted by the non-destructive power of ICT with its undo and incremental save facility. When there's high challenge and low threat and ICT is doing the scaffolding work, creative risk taking is underwritten by the cradle of a supportive environment. To make the most of the opportunity teacher expectations should be high.

Case study

Eight year olds and Flash: taking risks and learning – building graphical muscle
'Here in the classroom I see the students doing something difficult and succeeding. It's an activity where the creative rewards are high and their brains are starting to hurt a little. I ask what they are doing and most are able to articulate the challenge. One boy, using Flash animation software, describes the mathematical difficulty he is having to get the wheel to spin in the right direction as his cart moves across the screen, another tells me of the magical "multiple undo" command which allows you to go right back to where you started, should you need to.'
Geoff Dellow is a man on a mission. He is motivated by the opportunity to develop higher order thinking and problem-solving skills – to let learners have some fun in an environment of high challenge. He is in part driven by the potential sterility of an overly prescribed curriculum and he wants to make sure that challenging tasks of designing, developing and editing their own animations are learning opportunities increasingly available to students in primary schools across the subject barriers.

Teaching others – that magical trinity of doing, saying and showing – also helps to lock in the learning and allows students to work in their 'style of choice' for part of the time leading to that valuable learning state of 'focused attention' or immersion in the subject. New tools and networking capability with ICT have broadened the bandwidth and now provide a variety of ways in which this instruction of others can take place.

Perhaps the time is right to augment the arbitrary and artificial syllabus constructs and tap into the motivation that flows when we allow staff and students to build and share their own products of reflected experience and instruction before publishing them to share locally. 'Don't teach me let me learn,' says Prashnig (2002) – the next stage is giving learners the tools to finish the job and tell the story of their own learning in a number of different ways

Many schools see the potential of ICT as a production tool allowing teachers and students to 'learn by doing' in making their own learning artefacts for use by themselves and others. Perhaps once a term in each subject a student working alone or in a group should have the opportunity to submit a piece of work, resource or digital artefact to the central store/digital repository.

Activities and products can range across all subject areas

● Make your own daily radio news programme.
● Design, illustrate and publish your own German comic.
● Make your own history radio programme – hear it broadcast last thing on a Thursday as school finishes.
● Insert a clip of yourself into a piece of archive video footage on Home Front commentary from the war, talking about rationing, for the lunchtime video shorts competition.
● Animate a water molecule passing through a cell wall for the biology resource bank. See it used as part of a large (turbo-teaching) group lecture for students in Year 7 (visitors always welcome).
● Make your own feely bag relief map of Europe.
● Design a learning mat (an A3 'placemat' with pictures and text to recount the detail of a module). This could also contain individual targets to map out the learning and provide a visual and a textual roadmap through it.
● In a small team put together two key animations to show key learning points that have to be taught and understood, for example, peristalsis, continental drift, osmosis.
● Make an animated timeline of the last century.
● Produce a 'zoomagram' of the solar system starting in outer space and ending up at the road outside the school using flick-paper animation or software such as Flash.
● Make a 3D 'feelagram' of the liver – drawn by hand, scanned on the computer, labelled, then printed out and modelled and vacuum-formed in the CDT room.

There is a great deal of potential in schools developing their own resources leading from activities and reflections on their own learning. If this corpus is one that advertises its presence and is visible with occasional large wall-projected displays in a public place such as a library wall so much the better.

Many schools are seeing the value in doing and sharing it for themselves – building resources, publishing and broadcasting and sharing locally. For learning is a local, social experience. It's a more sensible model for schools to have an active role as producers and celebrators of their own shared knowledge, making use of new tools rather than adopting just the passive consumer approach to receiving information from a large central pool or grid. As schools look at remodelling their curriculum with the aim of bringing learning opportunities together with the in-house production of learning resources, the management and use of a wide range of media resources will be an issue.

 Most learning happens casually and even most intentional learning is not the result of programmed instruction.

Ivan Illich (1970)

The challenge for teachers, parents and all educators now is to find our own points of access with these tools and to resist the pressures which would see us all adopt common tools and approaches – the dead hand of uniformity has little place in the learning process. One size doesn't fit all and students can have opportunities to demonstrate their understanding in many media alongside text.

Telling stories and making things in clay or paper, sound, image and video formats are all obvious points of access. In curriculum terms this might translate into recording some sound files, making curriculum animations to demonstrate key principles and filming and editing a school news programme.

Getting the balance right

Getting ICT in its place sometimes entails giving some curriculum space and time to building and publishing learning resources and exemplars which serve to lock in the learning and let teachers and students see how they might use these tools in their own way in the future. Schools have enjoyed particular success with projects designed to build resources in the following areas. Think of these areas as five generic thinking and doing tools that can be adapted, extended and used across all curriculum subjects and age ranges. You can also make and share these rudiments across a variety of media types and resources.

➡ Running your own school radio station
➡ Building your own classroom animation studio (for making and sharing curriculum animations)
➡ Digital story-telling
➡ Building graphicacy
➡ Building a school television station

Each one of these can be seen as a natural extension of the work schools already do. Combining two or three such approaches can lead to a transformatory approach to building and sharing locally, for example, 'Here it's common for us to make and share our learning.'

Schools are viable communities in their own right

We will look at the medium of the internet as an accelerated learning tool in the next chapter but first let's look inwards and see what we can do within the school with these new tools and opportunities. For regardless of the rush to broadband connectivity – schools are and will remain viable communities within their own right. They already have very fast internal networks in place for the storage and transportation of sound and image alongside text. Communication within the school currently happens at up to 50 times the speed of a two megabit broadband connection that many schools possess to the outside world and the web. For schools with a modem link the speed of internal networks is up to 500 times faster. There will of course be exceptions but as a general rule of thumb it's often better for a learner to have something current and useful locally than something slow and out of date on the web. In one sense, it's best to think of the web as an offshore feeding ground and the school network as the primary learning and sharing learning point.

The following five projects are examples of how schools can use ICT to combine a range of learning styles using a number of accelerated learning approaches.

Breakthrough project 1

Run a school radio station across the school network for free: building the profile and management of sound recording as an accelerated learning tool within schools.

'I've just had a request in from Miss Jones in class 3'

Case study

Melike, a Year 9 student, looks confidently out of the window, ascertains the climatic conditions then turns to her microphone and goes straight into recording a confident weather forecast that is broadcast across the school network live as she speaks. 'Yes it's looking a bit grey and I think it's going to rain.'

The student hosting her own radio show is from Little Heath Special School, in Redbridge and the two pieces of software she is using – Winamp MP3 player and Shoutcast server software – are both downloadable from the internet for free. Later I will hear her run a 'spot the tune competition'. The school radio system housed in the classroom of ICT co-ordinator David Ware has been running for over two years now. 'It gives many of our children who have problems with text a chance to communicate in a medium where they have considerable mastery,' says David.

The radio uses the standard school network to 'broadcast' the sound out to all other machines on the system and any machine can be 'tuned in' just by clicking a link. 'Sometimes we use it in conjunction with the internal phone system so that students call the DJ's phone with their quiz answers or requests,' says David. At other times students broadcast the news and film reviews. Staff have even started to put together one minute homework help programmes that are broadcast at home time.

WEBSITE
WEBSITE

What you will need
A collection of sound files in MP3 format made into a list and a way of playing this list in a particular order – it could be Shoutcast (www.shoutcast.com) or iTunes (www.apple.com/itunes), both available for free from the internet.

Getting started
Step 1. First download or purchase some sound recording software that turns any recorded sound into waveform – a wave displayed on screen to show the pitch and amplitude of speech. Once you set the software to record and speak into a microphone, a waveform will appear on screen. Currently Audacity is the free waveform editor of choice (http://audacity.sourceforge.net).

WEBSITE

Step 2. The wave can then be edited, correcting mistakes and deleting 'ums' and 'aahs' if appropriate, and introducing effects such as echo and delay (try them and see). Many students relish the opportunity to provide a final edited fair copy from their own slightly rougher and less polished source material. This provides the auditory equivalent of video self-modelling where students end up with a perfection that never existed in reality but the process of producing it gives them the confidence and motivation to achieve closer to it next time.

Step 3. Once edited, the sound files need to be saved in a file format known as MP3 – this is a way of saving sound files that keeps the quality high but the physical file size low. The format also carries a certain cachet with learners as it's the file type music is stored in on the internet. Save your file into a folder with an appropriate name like 'Thursday history' so that it's easily recognizable.

Step 4. Finally, run some broadcast software and make a playlist containing the sound files you wish to use in the order you want to play them.

Extension
It may be useful to provide a sample bank of good performances in terms of audio commentary. Play some old audio commentaries to students so they can start to identify what makes a compelling recording broadcaster. The National Sound Archive housed in the British Library includes many older radio programmes and interviews (www.bl.uk/collections). Those interested in

WEBSITE

WEBSITE

pursuing the research further can make a 'listening appointment' via the internet and go and listen to a massive collection of human voice and music which the archive contains. The history site of www.collectbritain.co.uk (also at the British Library) provides another topical example with extensive audio archives telling the story of life in the past.

Sound recording software that lets you see and adjust the sound on screen is known as waveform editing. It allows students to speak, sing and so on and see the resulting sound file displayed on screen as a wave file – for years we have been saying 'I see what you are saying' and now we can!

In one sense, these are profound tools as they bring management and editing potential to human speech – one of our key functions as learners. The process is also high challenge–low threat as learners have the ability to identify and highlight errors and delete them from the final version. High challenge may also be found in the fact that Audacity and other similar software allows multi-tracking where a voice recording can be mixed with a backing track so that staff and students may produce and broadcast their own concert reviews.

A concert review is an accelerated learning technique where the voice is floated over and punctuated to the natural cadences within the music and achieves an intensity of memorable impact beyond words and music used separately.

Running a radio station – broadcasting audio files around the school network

1. The first key resource is some sound recording software such as Audacity or Sound Forge.
2. The second key principle is a list manager that allows you to add and edit MP3 files in a particular running order and plays through the sequence of sound files in the order you have arranged them. This software is usually combined with some broadcasting capability – some simple software that 'serves' the sound around the network where it can be heard on any machine on the network that has simple MP3 player software allowing it to 'tune in to the broadcast' – in this case, the IP 'postal address' of the computer on which the broadcaster software is situated.

Any school with three or four computers connected to each other using a simple box connector known as a 'hub' can run a radio station. Once in place and when instructed to play, the radio will broadcast all sound files in the playlist starting from the top line and working through all the files. The person running the radio station can then insert their live comments in between these files. All other computer stations with speakers or headphones attached can then tune into the broadcast. Wireless networking will make the process even simpler allowing one machine to broadcast and for other computers or servers to pick up and play the signal. Devices such as Airport Express now allow sound to be broadcast wirelessly to any speaker system. You simply plug the Airport into an electrical socket – it looks rather like a high tech version of a triple adaptor. Next connect it to a powered speaker system. Now with any wireless PC or Mac you can log onto the server the device provides and transmit your MP3 files for playing over the airwaves. Put such a device in the school hall connected to a power speaker and you have the bare bones of a school broadcast system.

Airport Express from Apple – plug it in, connect a speaker and send your MP3s wirelessly for playing

With software such as iTunes, you simply arrange your tracks in the order you want them to play and the software does the broadcasting for you.

I see what you're saying

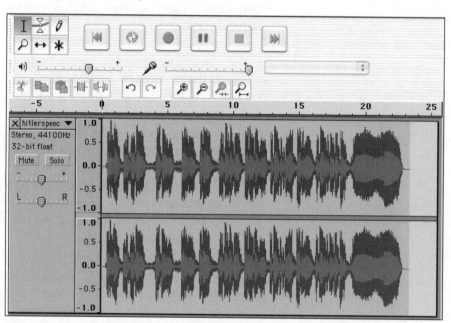

Many pieces of software now allow you to edit the waveform of your sound file (see Audacity stereo recording above) – the software may change but this basic principle will hold good.

Taking it forward

Start small but keep it regular

How we use these tools matters more than the transient capability of a particular piece of software. To break through the inertia trap try to present the radio in a certain place at a certain time each week, for example, a laptop in the dining hall linked to good quality speakers and playing through a previously assembled programme list of sound files could honestly be described as a 'school radio station' listening point. The benefits of regular repeated use is that after the third week children will remind you to do it – that's if it's caught on. If it hasn't, have a break and think about how these tools and approaches might be used in other ways. Run a short drop-in training for staff and students. Explain that the waveform editing process allows mistakes and delays to be edited out and encourage them to try recording in one-minute segments.

Ideas for radio programme content

- Music department compose jingles for school radio station.
- Students produce and record curriculum songs.
- One-minute shorts from the subjects — what is argon? – metaphors explained.
- Modern languages translate news from BBC website and make one-minute broadcast in French and German, delivered within 20-minute time frame.
- Deadline writing — students write summaries of breaking news for one-minute news slots.
- Sport and weather round-ups using the web for up to the minute research.

Finally, consider the use of audio files in the creation of a 'parent radio' channel, where primary schools can broadcast the school news at home time in four different languages. Even better, students who are learning English as an additional language and are not native speakers get to be the experts in this process.

Breakthrough project 2

Build a classroom animation studio

'Four more frames and that's a wrap – or at least a cape'

Animation, a close relative of film making, is the process of recording up to 24 still frames to produce a second of moving action. Due to a phenomenon known as 'persistence of vision' (where our eyes retain images for a tenth of a second), the individual images have the illusion of movement, and animators can bring objects to life.

Animation seems to be one of those magical areas with great potential to provide hands-on learning opportunities across the age and subject range. Perhaps this is not surprising as the process of animation combines the use of all learning styles – the visual, auditory, kinesthetic and tactile. Imagine a Victorian puppet theatre with 'characters on sticks' brought into the digital age where in the corner of the classroom there is a place where students can go to 'tell and record a picture story' of something happening over time. This might be an enactment of a historic event – the Battle of Hastings, the slow spread of linear town development, the passage of a water molecule through a partially permeable membrane or the process of digestion.

With props of plasticine, a plastic figure and a picture, you too can tell the compelling story of digestion

The potential of matching the process to the curriculum is almost endless – the value of the opportunity is that it allows students a concrete and tactile experience with the material they are studying. It's also of course another chance to hit the media shift key and get beyond text and talk. By occupying the hands you also free the mind and you'll notice how ideas, connections and conversation starts to flow.

Resourcing the animation studio is straightforward. Plasticine is still one of the most useful resources. Instead of characters on sticks, a visit to the local charity shop can provide plastic models, Playmobil and other plastic characters as props, and finally a cardboard box (about wine box size) provides the stage, proscenium and wings. Students usually enjoy painting their own backdrops or, alternatively, pictures can be printed from the web. Some teachers even film their animations to the 'live' backdrop of a laptop screen showing the relevant images.

The use of the simplest digital cameras allows a series of still pictures to be taken with the characters and props moving slightly between each still. Finally, use some image animation software to stitch the stills together and hey presto, you have an animation – a tool to tell a story about any curriculum content or principle.

Ideally the finished work should be saved as an animated GIF – a file format that will play in any web page on the school network and world beyond without any extra requirements or plug-ins. In one sense, it's the Esperanto resource for telling a picture story. You can keep the size of the file down by resizing the animation before finally saving to 320 pixels wide by 240 pixels high. Smaller files load faster and others are more likely to persevere and view your creation if it doesn't take too long to download.

Building your animation set
You will need the following items to build your studio:

➡ A simple three-sided cardboard box where students can design their own backdrop and lighting arrangement. This can be as simple as cutting a hole out of the side of the box and shining in a torch.

➡ The simplest of cameras can be used for animation, even the little eyeball cams ostensibly bought for video conferencing. Some schools set up a camera on a tripod to grab stills and this gives more consistency and can lead to a higher quality of animation The iStopMotion software (www.istopmotion.com) originally for the Apple Mac works well with a fixed camera.

➡ PaintShop Pro is one of the most useful pieces of software as after version 5 they built in a separate tool known as Animation Shop. The animation wizard within the software automates the animation process and takes less than a minute to produce the final results from a series of images.

WEBSITE

Teachers working on animation as a class project should note the importance of giving every member of the team a specific role: cameraman, lighting, props, producer, the one who has to bring it to the front of the class to premiere on the class projector attached to a computer as part of a visual plenary.

If the animation studio has a permanent place in the classroom it can be brought into lessons as the opportunity arises. Baileys Court primary in Bristol has allocated an area for animation in the corner of their ICT suite. Children are sent from lessons to make an animation as the need arises and the wall around contains posters of helpful prompts such as 'How can we use animation in our learning? Tell your teacher your ideas' and 'Remember to keep the camera in one position'.

Why animation might be a good idea

Quote from Ken Russell, 'I never liked school but I knew at 12 that I wanted to be a film director.'

Nick Park of *Chicken Run* and *The Wrong Trousers* fame has clear memories of only one day of his school life – the day the teachers gave him plasticine. His Dad gave him a camera and the rest is history.

Now a £400 camera and a laptop can give all students the opportunity that Ken Russell had to wait until he was 30 to achieve.

A fast-track way to unlock creativity for many students is to occupy the hands and free the mind and the mouth it seems. Activities such as animation also provide the space and time for the right side of the brain to get in on the act – to see what it can literally dream up.

Taking animation further

We know there's much curriculum potential for using animation – the place where image meets movement and time – but until now there have been few tools fit for classroom use beyond tools for making simple animated GIFs. Flash software from Macromedia is rapidly being accepted by the commercial world as the animation and web-authoring tool of choice because of its great flexibility of handling multimedia and logical programming. It's also very efficient at handling sound using the MP3 format to squeeze a lot of sound into a small file size. Simple sound and movement projects only require 10k storage space that means you could squeeze 150 multimedia works onto one floppy disc. Special education deals mean that Flash is now a cheaper option than any of the more limited multimedia software usually bought by schools.

Built around a timeline metaphor, Flash allows you choose what actions you want to achieve and place objects in various stage positions so that they move over time. Originally designed as a drawing package, Flash also features some unique graphic tools – if you draw a rough outline, Flash tidies it up and makes it look professional – children love this feature. Clickable buttons can be included to increase the control and interactivity and a large library of tutorials, graphics, sounds and templates is included as part of the software. Flash automates the process of animation so that once you have drawn a start and end point for your object, it will work out and insert all the in-between frames.

Flash is also useful 'VAKT ware' in that it allows you to keep the media range high, combining image, text and sound while keeping the file size low enough to assist the process of publishing on the web for others to see.

▌ Breakthrough project 3

Bringing story-telling back to the classroom: developing a digital story archive

Story-telling is still the best carrier medium we have for teaching. As a species, we have a deep psychological need for stories and now the bandwidth of the narrative skein we can weave is broadening. Image and sound have come alongside text.

From the US to the western seaboard of Ireland and from Stornaway to Soweto we are rediscovering the power of stories to engage, motivate and make learning memorable. The term 'digital story-telling' is used to describe the generic process of linking sound and music to a series of still pictures. In a way it allows us to take the oral tradition forward into the digital age and share narratives beyond live performance events. The approach could be described as 'less is more ware' as the restraint of using still images focuses attention on the sound and the overall effect is more engaging than straightforward digital video for many applications. 'PowerPoint for the soul' says Brendan Routledge, a support teacher working on digital story-telling projects with schools in Suffolk, UK.

The trick with ICT, at times, is to ask not what is possible but what is powerful? In engaging the senses and getting the message across, we remember things we feel strongly about and stories are something we usually can't resist responding to.

Digital story-telling is a new concept based on the old principles of story-telling. Using MovieMaker software, which is free with Windows XP, or similar video editing software like iMovie (free with Apple Mac computers), students record and edit their stories linking them to a series of still images using the record narration facility.

'iMovie software for the Apple Mac allows stills to be sequenced and synchronized with sound and music tracks'

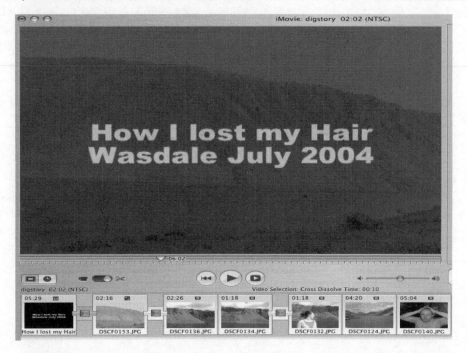

How to do some digital story-telling

➡ Decide on a story to tell.

➡ Start with pictures or talking stories.

➡ Record the sound and produce or procure some music.

➡ Add sound and synchronize it to the pictures.

Some dramatic work has been produced in schools. In one case, a boy who 'never usually got past writing his name' produced a detailed audio story with pictures on 'how I made my apple crumble'. Another example detailed the sad demise of a parrot called Roberto Baggio. The work provides a fast track to senses particularly when the spoken word is linked to images and mixed with music as a backdrop.

Taking it further

➡ Set up a few laptops/computers with scanners and invite older, local residents to bring in pictures taken of the area in the past.

➡ Get children to interview them about the pictures and their memories and then show them how their pictures are scanned.

➡ These interviews could also be recorded onto audio tape and later downloaded onto the computer. Some might wish to record straight onto the computer using Audacity or similar software. All the work could be stored in a folder on the network and included in a presentation launch.

➡ Combine the pictures with the voice recordings and music as part of a premiere in the turbo-teaching area.

Digital story-telling also has considerable potential as a mentoring and self-advocacy device. A number of projects are looking at the approach for enhancing records of achievement with digital story-telling especially for students with special education needs.

A digital story-telling transition project could feature the children telling the story of their lives, interests and aspirations for the future. These resources could then be featured during parents evening for new arrivals.

Useful websites

WEBSITE

http://clutch.open.ac.uk – Digital story-telling in local communities in Buckinghamshire.

Software which can be used:

WEBSITE
WEBSITE

MovieMaker for Windows XP (www.microsoft.com/windowsxp/downloads/updates) iMovie for Apple Mac (www.apple.com/ilife/imovie)

WEBSITE

or the Flash-based Photojam for either platform from www.shockwave.com

Breakthrough project 4

Building the muscles of graphicacy

Visual and graphical literacy is a key life skill in 'an age of too many words'. Many students are literate and numerate but still only able to draw like an eight year old at the time they leave school at 16. Teachers who wouldn't dream of saying they cannot write happily admit they cannot draw, yet much of the exposition and explanation they carry out would be more useful for many students if they were confident graphically and could show what they meant as well as saying it.

 Graphicacy is the ability to understand and present information in the form of sketches, photographs, diagrams, maps, plans, charts, graphs and other non-textual, two-dimensional formats.

F. Aldrich & L. Sheppard (2000)

The good news is that with space, time and the right support strategies (human and digital) we can all learn how to draw. In addition, many ICT resources now allow us to work with images with a little more ease and certainty.

In *Drawing on the Right Side of the Brain*, author Betty Edwards (1989) notes that 'Drawing is seeing …The magical mystery of drawing ability seems to be, in part at least, an ability to make a shift in brain state to a different mode of seeing/perceiving.' To read the world has been said to be a kind of madness, so it's essential that we continue to build the drafting and drawing capability as teachers and learners, for to communicate through illustration and graphical device is a fast track to understanding for many learners. Graphical representations of understanding, mind maps and symbolic representation have much to offer in getting the learning message across.

Learning to see differently

Gertrude Stein, as quoted in Edwards (1989), asked the French artist Henri Matisse whether when eating a tomato he looked at it the way an artist would. Matisse replied, 'No when I eat a tomato I look at it the way anyone else would. But when I paint a tomato then I see it differently.'

Six steps to graphicacy

➡ Give hand drawing a profile – create a gallery display area on the wall and on the internal network.

➡ Create still life drawing zones where silent looking and drawing is the order of the day.

➡ Get all staff introduced to scanners and comfortable in their use.

➡ Experiment with the use of graphics tablets and tablet PCs (if available) for tracing and drawing.

➡ Provide a variety of drawing and modelling media – pencil, felt tip, clay and tracing paper.

➡ Model good drawers by getting them to tell the class how they do it, perhaps at times coming to the front and drawing so others can see via an OHP, tablet PC or on the whiteboard.

The flatbed scanner is one of the most underestimated tools of our time. Looking like a photocopier that was not fed enough when it was young, the scanner works by copying the image from the page and taking it to the computer screen for further manipulation and development.

The digitizer pad is a low cost, pen sensitive pad where whatever you draw with a special stylus appears on the computer screen. The device is ideal for tracing – another 'part-reverie' layer of interaction with the subject – the greaseproof paper of the digital age.

Using the tablet PC brings back the hand as the ultimate input device and begins an end to mouse dominance, a tool that many teachers and learners find very spatially challenging and stressful.

Interactive whiteboard tools also provide key opportunities for graphical illustration and take the Rolf Harris effect (Can you guess what it is yet?) to the front of the classroom.

Case study

The artist's story

Spike Gerrell, the illustrator of some of the illustrations in this book, works first on his pictures away from the computer using an ink pen which he dips manually in the inkpot. 'It's a close relative of the quill,' says Spike. 'Nothing else seems to get the right genuine type of line.' Looking at the pictures you can see what he means – he wants a line 'with some of him in it' and even the most sophisticated stylus and digitizer pad would give him less that his trusty pen. Once the outline is complete, however, Spike has no problem scanning in the image and using Photoshop software to produce stunning graduated colour fills. This is an idea we can develop in the classroom – using the computer just to finish and share, with most of the creative and careful work and thought going on elsewhere between hand and eye and page.

From human hand to a screen near you – two stages of digital creativity

The slingshot effect in action

'Constraint is a turn-on for creative people,' said Björk (2002) during a BBC radio interview – it may also be a necessity for others to stop them getting lost in the endless opportunity of "the possible".'

Less is more – two activities

Take a piece of paper – fold it in half longways and again and again. Fold it again until you have 16 rectangles – cut them out and it means that a class of 32 can illustrate a subject on just two sides of A4, which can be scanned in less than a minute for storage and other digital enhancement or animation. Students will also enjoy the constraint of the small frame to draw in as opposed to the full page of A4.

Better quality drawing scale and colour seems to emerge when space is limited. Perhaps there is also a feeling of safety and the A4 format may be the enemy of graphical promise at times. Another way to limit the space available, is to draw a text box in a Word document and invite illustration within that space only.

Drawing is and will remain a skill best done by hand. This subtle interplay of hand and eye leads at times to insight and understanding. Leading UK mathematician, Sir Roger Penrose (2003) says that doodles can help with wrestling with highly abstract calculations and that 'you lose a lot when it is drawn on the computer…you gain more insights when you draw by hand.'

This picture (reproduced by permission of Geoff Dellow) was drawn by children of Newbury Park Primary School, Ilford, who were presented with the challenge of bringing the tableau of an African village to life.

First draw your village, then scan it in and animate a camp fire in the foreground – easy for an eight year old once their teacher has told them mistakes can be undone

The advent of the tablet PC will also help to extend this process of drawing while you talk as the teacher can write and draw by hand straight onto the computer screen. By adding a projector to the process, the image can be shown live on the big screen. With screen recording software like Captivate from Macromedia, drawing and voiceovers can be done on the computer before the lesson and played back and then stored for future reference.

Interactive whiteboards in turn also provide an opportunity to draw, illustrate and mark text and diagrams. Drawing skills will come to the fore for teachers wanting to get the most from this resource.

Graphicacy guidelines

➡ Think about holding a no writing day where all answers have to be spoken or drawn.

➡ Use the OHP and whiteboard to get images into students' visual fields – otherwise we just put words up and words don't tell stories so readily for many students – they bypass the visual memory.

➡ Get the art department to run a drawing and illustration drop-in session/module for other staff.

➡ To make illustration a regular part of their teaching teachers will need support to build their own skills in graphical representation. At times ICT can help with the scaffolding, support and undo opportunities they need when taking risks.

➡ Reinforce the use of the undo command and model the effect of layers by building up a drawing on various layers of plastic or cling film and show how one layer can be removed leaving the others untouched as a concrete example from the real world.

➡ Access to some quality graphics software is also essential, not a luxury. It would be unthinkable for teachers not to have access to a word processor and the same should be true of graphics. Photoshop, PaintShop Pro or CorelDraw are all examples of the type of graphics software that allow the key activities of cropping, colour adjustment and resizing to be carried out.

▌ Keep 'CLEAR' in your mind

Finally, we've developed a simple way of remembering the criteria to apply when selecting a graphic and assessing its usefulness as a teaching aid. This takes the form of a mnemonic:

C is for central point.

What is the purpose of the graphic? Is it just to make the page more attractive or does it give information not in the text?

L is for layout.

Is the graphic well designed and clearly presented? Does it do its job well? Is just the right-hand side of the image in use – has it been cropped for maximum effect?

E is for example.

Is the graphic a good example of its type? Can it be used to teach about graphics more generally?

A is for assumptions.

What prior knowledge is assumed of the viewer? What misconceptions might arise if these assumptions are not met?

R is for redesign.

If you are critical of the graphic, consider redesigning it yourself. How would you change it?

Adapted from F. Aldrich & L. Sheppard (2000)

Case study

The Australian education classroom behaviour specialist, Bill Rogers, draws out the scenarios as he talks about the various types of behaviour that are hard to manage in the classroom. By mixing voice, image and activity, the messages are reinforced and viewers find their own first point of access. It's a very powerful approach and one that become part of all teachers' repertoire and one we can all develop – live on a blackboard or whiteboard or on the screen via a stylus input on a tablet PC connected to a projector.

Graphical tune-up activities

➡ Holding a pencil in each hand, draw two different animals at the same time.

➡ Again, holding a pen in each hand, write your first name with your left hand and your surname with your right.

➡ Draw a building that you can see as it would appear if you were looking at it from the other side.

Get students to do these types of activities as an extension of cross lateral Brain Gym® type activity. Once again, it will provide a chance to go beyond text and writing. Occupy the hand – free the mind. Occasionally, get learners to talk about what they are doing while they are drawing. This helps to tap into deeper levels of reflection and understanding and some good drawers will provide insights that others will be able to learn from.

It is reported that 25 per cent of Royal College of Art students have some form of dyslexia compared with 10 per cent of the general population. Some suggest that people with some form of text reading difficulty often have superior visual and spatial abilities. Alternatively, it might be the case that if you are not good at communicating through words as a child you might persevere in building the skills which will allow you to communicate through pictures.

 If you are constantly told you have the wrong answer it must be a relief to find a sphere where there is no right or wrong answer. And the more you draw the better you get at it.

Oona Rankin (2003)

Bring movement to still images

Consider making a web gallery using the animated GIF of several pictures to do some story-telling around illustrations. Think about making your own 'Jackanory type' effect where the camera travels slowly around one large detailed illustration or photograph with audio voice-over or music. This rostrum camera approach is built into the Apple iMovie software, named after Ken Burns, a US cameraman, and the technique is very effective – another 'less is more' approach using the still to maximum effect.

Hand drawn, computer scanned and then taken further using graphics software

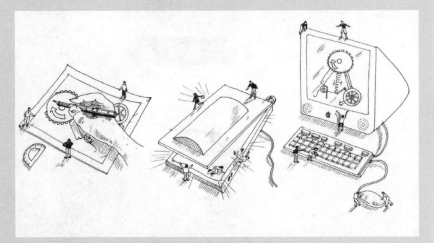

Getting the most from the scanner

➡ Start by running your graphics program.

➡ Choose 'file aquire'.

➡ In the settings options make sure dpi (dots per inch) is set to 70, 75 or 90. If you scan at higher resolutions you will end up with large file sizes, and they won't look any better on screen or when printed. You would only scan at a higher resolution if you were sending a picture out for high quality printing in a school brochure for instance.

➡ Choose 'preview' to see a thumbnail (a small image) of your image.

➡ Use the mouse to drag the 'cross hair' around the bit of the image you want to scan.

➡ Now select scan.

Ideas for activities

➡ At subject level, illustrate your own comic – give students photocopies of a comic page with the dialogue erased before copying and blank out some scenes for them to fill in the gaps.

➡ Give a pictures homework – where students have to annotate an image, for example, label this glaciated terrain with drumlins, eskers and erratics.

➡ Use collage and comparison tasks – compare two images of childhood, what do they tell you about life in the 1940s?

➡ Take a digital picture of the students and paste them in as heads on figures in a medieval painting, perhaps downloaded from the extensive art collection at the Web Museum Paris (www.ibiblio.org/wm).

➡ Use PowerPoint to label a picture using the 'autoshape' command and animate them so new labels are introduced each time the computer mouse is clicked.

WEBSITE

First test the students' knowledge, then have the labels appear

▊ Breakthrough project 5

Run a school television station

Certainly with radio and increasingly with digital video, the 'plumbing for distribution' is already in at school level. This provides the opportunity to turn on the tap of creative use across the computer system and bring sound and image alongside text in the digital learning diet.

In an ideal world and with long-term planning of cross-curricular ICT projects, I suggest that video is left alone until projects using radio and animation are well established. Video work is more expensive in terms of hardware costs and curriculum time taken than all the other approaches outlined in this chapter and sometimes the ends do not justify the means. That said, many schools have invested in the equipment and getting the finished video work to an audience via the network is a key way of increasing its potential use.

One way to make a start is to begin building a storehouse of digital video clips. The archive boom means that several major holders of video and film archive material are now busy digitizing and making content available online. The media archive warehouses possess exemplar material for students' raw material which they can use to experiment with, replacing sound tracks or adding voice-overs to change and enhance meaning.

WEBSITE

Some teachers are even showing students how they can drop their own freshly recorded footage into historical recordings, giving students a unique immersive approach to their subject. In a sense, it's the digital video equivalent of putting a student face on an historical figure from an old painting then getting them to write about what it felt and looked like in those times. Still and moving footage from the past is now easily available to many schools. Resources like Pathe (www.pathe.co.uk) and SCRAN (www.scran.ac.uk) are now provided free to many schools through their local broadband network.

Little Heath Special School students, Redbridge, UK, tell their own compelling account of the life of Anne Frank to a backdrop of original war footage (reproduced by permission of David Ware)

School television

Twenty years ago, Sharnbrook High School in Bedfordshire, UK had insufficient space to accommodate all students for a regular, full-school assembly. The head, Geoff Grounds, had the idea of putting a television in every classroom and broadcasting live each Monday morning to all classrooms. 'We are just going over live to the drama studio for the week's assembly with the headmaster.' From there it was a short step to send 'television crews' of students to video school sports fixtures at the weekends and these were then edited and broadcast to classrooms as part of a multimedia assembly. Less disruption of the learning day and a realization from students that they could be media makers rather than consumers were two of the initial benefits that Geoff noted. It's ironic that 20 years on such applications are still rare although every school has a network down which video could easily travel.

The first stage is to get a simple plumbed in way of recording – a place where you can go and be sure a camera will be connected and set up. Some schools are starting to set up a studio in an old book cupboard with a glass window to the corridor so that students can see recording in action (when the curtain is not drawn).

Another issue for schools wanting to develop this area is that there are a range of file formats for saving and broadcasting digital video clips. The international standard file format for digital video is known as MPEG, but a number of generic offerings exist and these can cause compatibility issues. If a movie is made and saved on an Apple Mac using iMovie, the export option is as a QuickTime file, a format developed by Apple but also available for PCs running Windows or Linux.

WEBSITE

WEBSITE

WEBSITE

WEBSITE

Apple QuickTime format for video has much to recommend it as clips can be saved from the internet to the desktop at the click of a mouse and the professional version of the software (currently £25 from www.apple.com/quicktime) allows the cutting and pasting of sequences between QuickTime clips. Some schools are using QuickTime Pro to great effect, downloading trailers of the latest movies and allowing students to film and paste in their own sequences and add voice-overs. Many schools have commented on how useful it is to be able to download video clips and resources in QuickTime format from the curriculum demonstration site www.ncaction.org.uk and play them offline whenever required.

Digital video guidance

➡ Get video clips into a common format that can be broadcast around the school network. The most straightforward of digital video format at present is Apple QuickTime (www.apple.com/quicktime). With the professional version, you can copy, cut and paste clips and carry out simple linear butt edits (where one clip is cut up against another – good enough for most television and film productions – you rarely see a fade or a dissolve in-between scenes in a television soap).

➡ Consider using software such as Live Channel that allows live camera work to be spliced with existing clips so that a student could introduce recordings before they are broadcast (www.channelstorm.com).

➡ Set up stations around the school network to tune into the broadcast using little cardboard cut-out televisions to overlay the screen and ask students 'do you want to be on your school television?'

Every school a mini BBC?

Case study

Colbayns High School

Health education is the focus for a Year 7 lesson at Colbayns High School, Essex – a large secondary comprehensive for 11–18 year olds. Phil Longshaw, head of the school's creative media and arts faculty, uses digital video as a standard instructional and analysis tool. Students devise storyboards for subjects such as bullying, relationships and drugs. These are then developed into drama sequences and recorded and edited in the school's mini editing suite. Once the video has been digitized, it is then broadcast over the school network using Live Channel software. This software allows students and teachers to select and cue a number of clips and acts a bit like a television studio on screen. The school have demonstrated this practice at BETT (British Educational Technology Show) for the last two years under the title 'BETT Goes to the Movies' and have provoked a good deal of interest both for the technical expertise of the students and the curriculum fit they have found for the tool of digital video.

Just imagine

The director sits in her studio. A delectable bank of monitors with live video feeds awaits selection at her whim. 'Fade to four then go in close on three please cameraman I and cut!' We know the language, but we've never had the opportunity to use it in context, until now. Yes, that visceral 'in the moment learning' opportunity of recording, cueing, editing and running your own television studio, once a joy reserved for the few, now looks as if it could be open to any school.

Case study

Roman ruins

Digital video is a versatile medium, so much so that it enabled Parkhill Junior School, in Essex, to share and learn from a special one-off drama experience.

Alison Seagrave, the school's ICT co-ordinator, wanted to make sure that all the work staff and students put into a history module last summer about the Roman invasion was not wasted. As part of their work on Romans this term, Year 4 has developed a four-part story. Each class took one part of the story and, working together, developed a screenplay and script so they could act out and film their part of the story.

'After a lot of hard work, some head scratching and, it has to be said, some fun, each class succeeded in putting together their part of the play,' says Seagrave. They began by producing a rough draft, which they then edited before making a book to put their finished work in. Initially, the children were shown how to use a simple hand-held movie camera from Intel. In ICT, the children used the camera to shoot small film scenes prior to the actual filming of the story. This helped them to devise camera angles.

In addition to planning, children were also encouraged to consider how they might film the event to best tell the story. The allocation of roles was another area of classroom management that Seagrave considered as the filming approached. 'We had a "director", "sound man" and "camera crew" for each scene,' she says.

With the support of two teachers, the final footage was edited by the students. The software used for this was iMovie on an Apple Mac. Finally, a QuickTime file was produced to enable the film to be shown over the internet and burned onto a CD-ROM. Copies of the CD-ROM were provided for parents, containing the final version of 'The Romans' and 'Parkhill Bloopers' – a series of out-takes from the production.

'The best bit about it all was that we were able to share with parents the time and effort taken to make the film and also the huge amount of learning that the children experienced,' Seagrave says. 'This work has now been embedded into the Year 4 curriculum, and next year's movie topic will be the Tudors.'

Second chance learning

The result of the Tudors project has been excellent ('If you're not satisfied with a scene you can do it over again until you are. And if you find it hard to read a text you can learn it by heart'). This work has served to strengthen the students' self-confidence which in turn has increased their progress in the subject.

The point about the best examples of digital video work in schools is that it doesn't need to be state of the art use of video editing what's important is the learning opportunities it provides: the autonomy, the spatial challenge of seeing through the camera's eye rather than your own and the clear sense of audience which underpin these projects. There is much potential in blending a combination of curriculum need, strong sense of audience and manageable time frame technology as catalyst – 'teachnology' has struck!

Taking it further

➡ Run a 'director's cut' competition with voice-overs on existing digital video clips.

➡ Launch film premieres in the turbo-teaching zone (see Chapter 5).

➡ Invite video professionals in to provide master classes in sound video and editing techniques for staff and students. For example, a school might hire an independent television producer to film good practice and also to work with staff explaining the processes and approaches so they could do something similar albeit at a lower level of competence in the future.

Chapter 4

Sharing the learning recipe in school and beyond

Moving beyond 12 month smart

At the end of each year do all the displays get taken down, the learning forgotten? Do the brilliant performances at drama, sport and public speaking seep away into the ether, filed in the folder marked 'forgotten' or do they 'vanish into the air from whence they came'? Twelve months later do teachers have to start from scratch without an exemplar to model or an idea from past achievements to inspire new learners?

In September or whenever your school year starts, does the learning have to begin all over again? Or can you go to a laptop wirelessly networked and access some artwork from four years ago – listen to a song from last year's play or an MP3 performance from last year's GCSE music? The opportunity to store and relearn from past experience is another of the illusory areas of ICT promise that teachers are now making tangible.

A key evolutionary moment occurs in the life of the school when more than three or four members of staff share a loose understanding of the concept of a shared folder – a place where worksheets and examples of pupil work can be placed so that they are accessible to all yet protected from deletion and change.

The defining moment however is when they move beyond awareness and into action. As staff contribute and critical mass is reached, the resource takes off. For, remember, schools are coherent communities in their own right and 'if you build it the audience will come'. Until we reach the point of easy regular local sharing we are, in one sense 'outside smart and inside stupid' as far as the digital access to resources is concerned. Now that's not a good way to be because learning is still a local social process.

If a teacher can't put a worksheet, a picture or a sound on the network and know that students can access but not alter it – then some of the most creative uses of ICT as a motivational and 'second chance learning tool' are ended before they begin. An ideal way to lower stress for learners is to show what good learning has looked like in the past.

Teachers need the same conceptual overview of the school computer network that they have of the photocopier – they can't fix it but they know how it works and how to ask someone about how they can take it further. In short, they need to have what we might call a 'vocabulary of expectation' and that's a precious and sometimes a hard won thing. Again, the locus of control needs to be close – within the school to start with rather than devolved to the local authority.

Easy email access for staff to send messages and a shared folder on the network where work such as lesson plans may be published and shared are two of the biggest contributions ICT can make to quickly reducing staff workload.

Four steps to sharing centrally

1. Build the sharing pot fast – don't mention intranets unless it's going to help understanding or development. Call it a shared area or something with a similar idea – descriptive but low threat. Talk about it first as a staff area for admin, lesson plan template worksheet storage; think about exemplification and student publishing over time.

2. Make sure staff are happy and confident about placing and retrieving work in the shared area – time spent making sure all staff are confident with where things are and what the various pots and/or folders are called on the network is time well invested if purposeful, confident work is to follow.

3. When the 'sharing pot' has developed enough to need a front menu and index you can give it a more 'grown-up name' – call it an intranet or Eric or whatever works for you and your staff to capture the idea of sharing and developing resources on a hard drive.

4. After some time you might consider putting part of the developing corpus online for the wider world out on the internet as a tool for students, parents and the wider school community.

Local sharing – switching on the amplifier

It's when we share, publish, show, tell and then get feedback that we can move into that fertile, iterative loop allowing us to do it better, faster and differently next time.

The use of local publishing on paper for display, onto CD-ROM or into a shared area on the network for others to see is part of the key to connecting the learning and tapping into the motivation – the 'wanting to learn stage' as Professor Phil Race describes the moment of learning onset.

Making the most of paper

In the area of print and technology, we see many delightful resonances of the past. Caxton set his first type in 72 points to the inch, the same measurement we still use today on our word processors.

The vestigial swirls and feet on many fonts, known as serifs, also have a distant historical connection for these stops and flourishes on letter shapes were to stop the chisel mark splitting any further when the letters were originally carved into stone. The space between lines on our digital screens is still called the 'leading' in memory of the lead spacers used to create the same effect with mechanically composed type. Students enjoy exploring this resonance of the past in our current tools and processes – such stories help them to understand the past and how we can learn from it.

Case study

How to keep line length to 65 characters

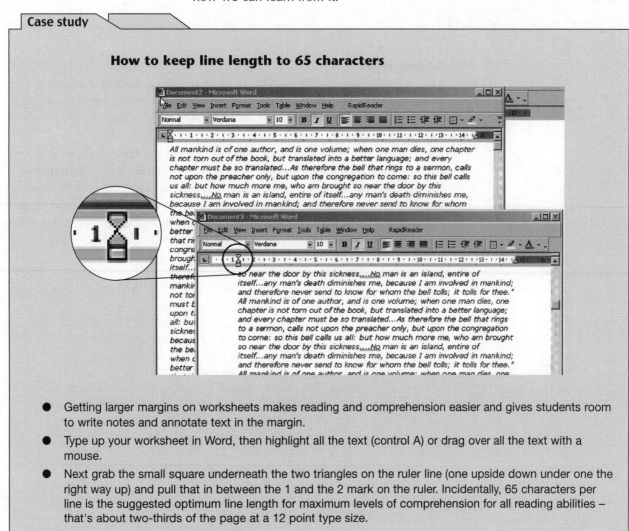

- Getting larger margins on worksheets makes reading and comprehension easier and gives students room to write notes and annotate text in the margin.
- Type up your worksheet in Word, then highlight all the text (control A) or drag over all the text with a mouse.
- Next grab the small square underneath the two triangles on the ruler line (one upside down under one the right way up) and pull that in between the 1 and the 2 mark on the ruler. Incidentally, 65 characters per line is the suggested optimum line length for maximum levels of comprehension for all reading abilities – that's about two-thirds of the page at a 12 point type size.

Case study

Leaving hidden messages in Word

The 'comment' feature in Word is powerful and underused. To add a comment, highlight the piece of text you wish to annotate by clicking and dragging the mouse over it. Next, choose 'insert' from the file menu and select the 'comment' option on the sub-menu that appears.

The same feature can be used on cells in an Excel spreadsheet. It's a useful way of explaining what's going on in cells which carry key formulae – when the student points the cursor at the relevant cell, an annotation box appears.

Thumbnail image of a page with major style attributes

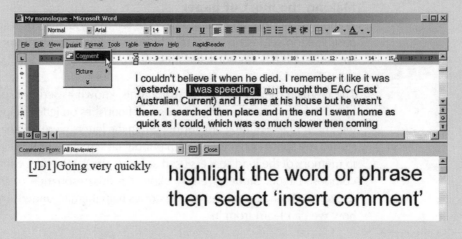

Design issues

It is a right of every teacher and learner to have an occasional attack of fontitis and to use fonts just because they are available; over time however restraint is necessary if clear communication on paper is to be achieved.

The type of font used and consideration of spacing and house style for standard documents all make a contribution to reading, comprehension and retention. A serif type face (where the letters have little feet and swirls) is usually found to be easier to read. Research shows that using serif fonts can boost reading speed by seven to ten words per minute. In one study it boosted comprehension by over 300 per cent when compared to work rendered in a sans serif font.

The end of upper case as we know it

CAPITAL LETTERS

SOMETIMES IT'S
HARDER TO READ US

YET SO MANY
NOTICES USE
US

ALL WE ARE
SAYING...

is give lower-case a chance

The management maxim, 'If you can't justify what you are doing, stop doing it', holds true for punctuation change and drift. We may be about to witness the end of capitalization as we know it. There seems to be no benefit to the use of all-capital communication in schools. For all learners, capitalization cuts the speed of reading. Why not devise your own classroom action research test to check this contention.

Sharing the recipes of what works on the page

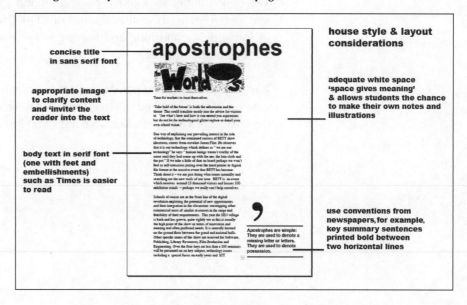

'Print is the prime instructional medium in our schools but not outside it,' said McLuhan (1962). Anyone who stands beside a photocopier in a secondary school in the UK, Australia or the US will be struck by the prophetic accuracy of these words and find ample evidence that we are still clearly in the age of the photocopier. Some teachers are 'photo copyists black belt third Dan'.

Several larger schools now copy over two million pages per year. As well as reflecting on the environmental impact and cost, it's a good idea to occasionally stop and ask how much of this provides good learning opportunities.

Some considerations on the printed pages we make in schools

➡ Images are often downgraded by copying.

➡ Colour – a vital part of the learning communication and aid to engagement and retention – is lost.

➡ A4 is often too large and too wide for easy reading if the text goes the whole way across the page. Size and colour matter more than we know but not always in the way that we think – ICT gives us low cost colour if read on screen, connections to the web (hyperlinks), movement and interaction.

➡ Use a variety of paper sizes for handouts – ask students for their preference of size and colour.

➡ Use minificates – tiny 2 cm square pieces of paper printed or handwritten with accolades and awards

➡ The dilemma of leaving white space on the page could be characterized as the 'environmentalists' lament' for there seems to be a correlation between wasting trees and helping learners; without space around them text and diagrams lose much of their meaning.

The opportunities for internal publishing and sharing in school include paper and web formats, as well as the use of CD-ROM. We look backwards as well as forwards – publishing and sharing is not just about the shared folder, the intranet or the internet.

It is worthwhile asking parents how they want to receive information, as often when parents are asked in what format they would like the school newsletter, the answer is 'on paper'. But what if it's 500 images from the field trip to Arran?

Case study

A revision tool taken further with group annotation, provides a reminder for students to browse and review

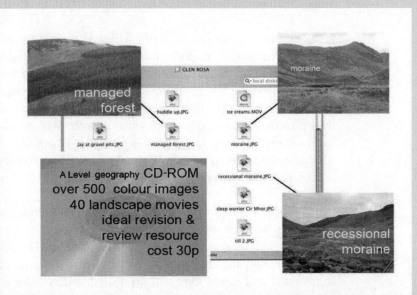

Screenshot reproduced by permission of Geography department, St John Henry Newman School, Stevenage

Over time, schools will consider CD duplication capability alongside that of the photocopier. For as little as 20p it's possible to give each student a beautifully illustrated CD-ROM resource complete with audio annotation.

Duplicating machines can now churn out fifty CDs in an hour

Why hasn't every school got one? Cost of replicating and distributing 1,000 pages is 20p versus photocopying costs of £10

The journey towards getting confident with electronic publishing, and schools' role within this, is a journey which will, at some point, involve all schools using electrons on the screen opposed to carbon on paper. The important thing to remember is that the journey should be guided by fitness for purpose – what's needed rather than what's possible.

It looks like we are finally about to leave the age of the photocopier and crossover to a more digitally integrated future. In *Fulfilling the Potential*, a booklet detailing the government's follow-up vision to the National Grid for Learning initiative, Ministers note that next steps 'will require every school to become e-confident'. The truth is close to the fact that pure economic necessity will take us towards an e-future since all schools are now connected to the internet and an email to a parent is free. At Netherhall School in Cambridge, all communication to parents is emailed as well as sent by post and the post option is under review – the certain shape of things to come.

As resources migrate from the page to the screen, management organization and rigour become more important. An example of this can be found in the area of digital images. Many schools have substantial banks of images gleaned from scanners, digital cameras on field courses and so on. If these are catalogued and stored they will be available down the years and across the subject areas in ways their original creators never imagined.

> **Making the most of digital images resources over time**
> Digital cameras should have proper date settings as this information is carried over into the digital file and becomes a useful asset when searching for images. Images should be indexed and stored by keywords for if they reside on a hard disk with a camera generated numerical name, they are only of use to the person who took them and only until they forget what the numbers relate to!

In a concluding letter in the first printed book in English – *Recuyell of the Histories of Troye* – William Caxton (1475) described how he had laboured on his translation of the text and how useful the new technology of print was.

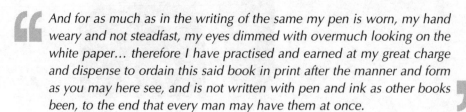

And for as much as in the writing of the same my pen is worn, my hand weary and not steadfast, my eyes dimmed with overmuch looking on the white paper... therefore I have practised and earned at my great charge and dispense to ordain this said book in print after the manner and form as you may here see, and is not written with pen and ink as other books been, to the end that every man may have them at once.

Although talking about the potential of the new printing technology, Caxton could have been talking about the intranet – the great potential of digitally stored resources is that the original copy remains even when a thousand learners have each taken their own copy away.

Intranets – building the wisdom within

There will always be a tension between the worldwide connections now possible for schools and the local sharing and celebration of work and achievement on internal networks via an intranet. One key future challenge for all schools in the next five years is to achieve their own balance between linking outwards and building their own intranets within.

Many schools have now made the intranet the fulcrum for sharing resources for learning and a repository for a variety of learning materials linked to a specific learning style.

Case study

Building a storehouse of local knowledge

A visionary headteacher and staff at Cramlington School, Northumberland have built the school's ICT around the latest research on the Accelerated Learning Cycle and all Year 9 lessons in all subjects are on the intranet. This means that each learning topic is connected to previous work and resources include visual and auditory points of access. Three graduate web designers are employed full-time in building and managing the intranet, which is accessible at speed from all 700 networked computer stations around the school. A full-time video technician helps teachers to film and digitize video clips and a dedicated video server has space for 4,000, ten-minute clips stored in the digital video AVI format. Teachers also make their own audio commentaries to accompany images and text files online. Over 80 interactive whiteboards are now in use in the school so teachers are confident that they can access these resources whatever their location – a cohesive whole-school approach built around a common system.

The work on learning styles in the school sits powerfully alongside this large investment in ICT and an intranet brimming with over 25,000 visual and auditory learning resources, many of them produced in-house – for learning is primarily a local experience.

'For new technology to transform education it must accompany new thinking on teaching and learning,' said Mark Lovatt, the deputy head.

Small, local gathering and sharing seems to work where large, online building of content and e-learning schemes have, so far, been less successful.

The ill fated e-University, recounted by John Naughton, shows what happens when the tail of technology wags the dog of learning.

> *…which when translated means that the e-University farce is being abruptly terminated. This is an excellent decision, but it comes too late to save the £30 million of public money which has been squandered on a venture that should have been strangled at birth. In the course of its brief but expensive existence, the e-U[niveristy] managed to recruit a total of 900 students worldwide, which works out at about £33,000 per student. Given those numbers, it would have been cheaper to have given each of these folks the money and sent them to Harvard.*

John Naughton (2004)

Schools can now be their own producers and publishers of content across a variety of media. Why not think of schools as if they were their own mini BBC service. Remember to get the branding and house style established early and add 'this production was brought to you by… ', at the end of every resource. In one sense, Geoff Grounds with the Sharnbrook television broadcasts (see

Chapter 3) was making intranets 20 years before intranets were invented using the appropriate carrier medium of the time – the local broadcast of television signals. Such powerful ideas will ride again – the networks are already in place – as we think outside the office paradigm and think of school as a supermarket, a mini BBC – making, sharing and learning.

Questions for local knowledge systems

Simple questions to ask and planning to consider:

➡ Can I share work easily?

➡ Can I publish work so that students can access it but not change it – so that they save their own developed version as a separate file?

➡ Can I make screen recordings and save templates?

➡ Are admin staff and classroom support assistants part of the publishing team and trained at publishing to the local corpus?

➡ What further skills are needed to support the development of such a resource?

➡ Another benefit of shared ideas, shared practice and shared resources is that these may in turn support collaborative teaching approaches as we will see when we get to the turbo-teaching zone.

Pneumatic communication

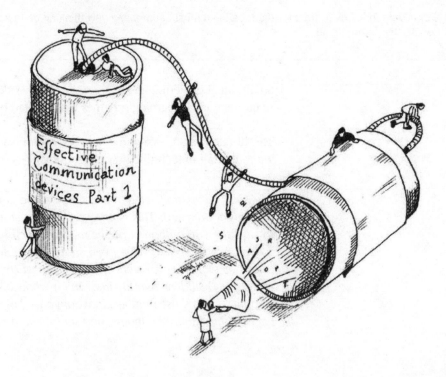

If ICT can't help us communicate better even over small distances within schools, let's go back to the tin cans and waxed wires or hose pipes and funnels communication – they were a better kinesthethic device in any case.

Web page – the carrier bag of our time

It's as if we have entered the age of the digital Victorians with the echoes of the classification surge carried out by famous botanists, geologists and engineers. Now schools are starting to develop their own taxonomies of resources, classifying, seeking connections and bringing order to mixed and disconnected materials. The aim downstream is to escape the incoherence of the possible – making the most of what we have by recording and indexing and therefore making it searchable and reusable perhaps in ways we had never thought of.

Gathering, growing and naming in the nursery of digital potential

Expect the unexpected

You will know you are close to success in local resource publishing when others start using resources you have published in ways that you never intended.

Regardless of the hype surrounding intranets, the core issues are simple to understand and, given even limited funding, to develop. As soon as a school has a network – a series of points around a school into which computers may be plugged – it has this potential to publish and share a local corpus of resources. The age of the digital maverick also beckons – just as we have no control over how teachers might actually teach, so we should actively seek to ensure no central body might control how individual schools deploy the use of ICT in their classrooms and broader community.

Digital Esperanto is the order of the day – if sharing matters (and it does) then we need to find the Esperanto files that everyone else can access.

Useful file types for intranet use:

 JPEG   *a picture – small size but good quality*

 MP3   *sound file – small size in memory terms but good quality and plays over the network without stuttering – ideal for school radio broadcasts*

 PDF   *a portable document format which keeps pages just right for print every time*

 SWF   *Flash file, sound, animation and interactivity in a tiny size package so that it opens quickly even across the internet – ideal way of packaging resources for home and community access, including sound and moving images*

 .mov   *(QuickTime movie) – save, cut and paste digital movie media with the QuickTime Pro upgrade*

 .wmf   *(Windows Media File) – a proprietary format for movies with Windows*

The connected page

'A computer not connected to the internet is like a brain without a spinal column.' Overheard from a primary student during interactive project research in Bristol.

As early as 1973, the first designs of the internet had been created. These specifications described how small 'packets' of information could travel between computers around the world, each with their own unique 'postal address', also known as Internet Protocol (IP). The next big breakthrough came in 1990 when Tim Berners-Lee invented the 'web page' – a way to link information together using 'hypertext'. The web page is the electronic echo of the printed page, but with an important difference – the underlined text, usually highlighted in blue and known as hypertext, forms clickable areas allowing the user to follow connections to new pages of information.

Tim Berners-Lee (1998), credited as being the designer of the world wide web which was to become the main communication medium for the internet, notes:

> *The dream behind the web is of a common information space in which we communicate by sharing information. Its universality is essential: the fact that a hypertext link can point to anything, be it personal, local or global, be it draft or highly polished.*

Susan Greenfield, director of the Royal Institution, has often noted that 'understanding is based around our ability to see and make connections'. The web provides the scope for connected learning where the relationship between individual ideas can be articulated and explored, where concepts can be examined in their hierarchical order, where depth is possible by drilling down into associated references.

The web page is the Banda Spirit master of our times. Those teachers old enough to remember the Banda duplicating machine will understand why I pause here for a moment of olfactory nostalgia. The Banda was an easy way to be a publisher. Similarly, web pages allow everyone to be a publisher with the benefit that they can store still or moving images and sounds with no extra effort.

'Slip inside the eye of your mind'

'Don't look back in anger', Noel Gallagher

New software tools like mind-mapping software help us to think in a non-linear way. Some of us who have sat through a very long PowerPoint presentation will have felt the limitations of this linearity. Thinking, for many of us, is also about associating and accommodating new ideas. The internet is a place of multiple, branching connections. These web links also serve as a metaphor for the internal workings of memory. A publishing revolution is now well underway where, as a key means of communication, we see carbon and ink challenged and increasingly replaced by electrons on the screen.

Using the internet brings forward two big opportunities – finding out information and communicating ideas. For many teachers, the most profound development of the last five years has been the sudden opportunity to tap into a bigger brain, and a larger gene pool of minds – to be able to gather, distil and adjust digitally available resources with their own learners' needs in mind.

Beyond the 13 inch window

Developing the skills of using the internet effectively is like building muscle tone. It comes with the exercise of seeing, doing and reflecting on the results. To build the muscles of effective use with the internet, students need to be shown how to tap into valid resources from trusted sources. As with any journey there are useful skills to learn that can help avoid the pitfalls. Knowing how to judge the integrity of information found on the internet is a key skill in the information age. The information age teacher needs both to make available trusted sources and to educate learners so that they themselves can read the runes of the trustworthy source.

Key critical pointers for the internet-wise learner are:

➡ What does the web address tell me about the site?

➡ What evidence do we have to support the views that are expressed?

➡ For what purpose was this resource produced?

➡ What evidence do we have that we can trust the validity of this source?

➡ What evidence do we have that the views expressed are objective, honest and fair?

➡ What else do we need to know in order to make use of this information?

Working out where a web page comes from

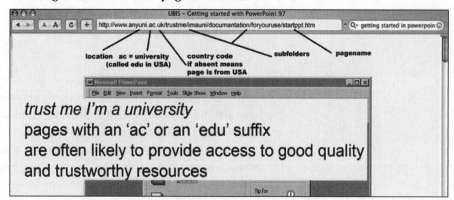

Nothing you will learn in the course of your studies will be of the slightest possible use to you in later life – save only this, that if you work hard and diligently you should be able to detect when a man is talking rot, and that, in my view, is the main, if not the sole purpose of education.

John Alexander Smith (1914), speech to Oxford University students

To adjust the above quote we might say that it still holds true and a key skill of internet use is to detect what is rot and what is not.

Building appropriate learning strategies

The internet is a living network of information waiting to be used rather than just studied. What follows are some thoughts about practical ways to use the resource of the internet in the classroom.

Too much early use in schools has perhaps been concerned with getting the internet installed and in giving students their turn at the terminal. As a new tool, it's understandable that many of us have been beguiled into confusing access with learning. While at times there is a value in exploration and the random following of connections, it could be construed as aimless browsing. At times, a more structured approach may help to build appropriate and purposeful use.

Even young learners can learn how to inform others and achieve much in the process. A simple rota can allocate responsibilities for printing out key resources on a daily basis for notice board display. The daily weather image, for instance, captured from a satellite spinning in space, can then be displayed in the entry hall for all to see. This ebb and flow from the virtual to the real and tangible helps learners see the potential for information when it is printed, articulated and shared.

Another useful approach to the internet is to consider it as a learning and thinking tool and coach students in effective use through a series of learning activities. These could include time-limited challenges to provide a target for efficient thinking. This approach could also help make shared resources go further. For example, allocating five minutes to gather all useful information on a subject. Some schools issue a two minute use voucher, or place a chess clock beside the internet search station for this purpose.

A clearly defined mini-research task can clarify the stages in finding, forming and framing information. Such activities help to move pupils away from simply cutting and pasting information, into thinking about what it means and how it can be used. Starters might include preparing a short presentation on:

➡ The purpose of different types of nets used by fishermen

➡ What was it like to send a letter in the 1800s?

➡ What were Faraday's key contributions to science?

➡ Why is Greek tragedy relevant to today?

➡ What kind of drink is 'port' and what is its history?

Then the teacher can discuss with students what type of research and subject matter the web is good for and where it is less efficient. This idea can be developed, for example, by using 'Mission Impossible' or a similar soundtrack to test research skills – by the time the music is finished your search time is up.

Search boards and the deferment of gratification – making the questions explicit

A way of making students 'think before they surf' is to place a small whiteboard in the resources area and call it a 'search board' or a similar name of your choice. Students are asked to articulate what it is they want to find before they undertake the search. The other half of the board then allows anyone who has information relating to the request to give advice.

How to defer gratification in the digital age

Introducing a time-lapse between declaring a query and carrying out the search provides further benefits. Pupils check the board and see if anyone has been able to come up with a better alternative source to the internet. Students can learn the protocol for exercising judgement in where answers may lie to a given question because the internet is not a comprehensive index to human wisdom. The best source could be Mr Jones because he was present at the time of the target event. We might even direct attention at times to 'coherent but forgotten' resources, such as the *World Book Encyclopedia* sitting on the shelf behind the computer.

We need to guard against students thinking that the internet is the repository for all that is important, for the greater part of human experience lies within our minds and in our experiences, and much of that will never be enshrined within the confines of a set of web pages. We must encourage our learners to think first, to evaluate the information that they discover, and to use it as source material for shaping into new knowledge.

Building bookmarks

To share good quality, trustworthy sites between staff, students and the wider school community is to invite others into our electronic library and to tap into a larger brain. Pointers to recommended websites, also known as bookmarks, act as the distillate of the community's online experiences. A set of bookmarks from a trusted source about useful websites contributes to the shared knowledge base of the school. In one sense, bookmarks are an algorithm of common experience – refined through hours of explorations and false alleys into a trusted corpus – valuable only if updated. The one tool that is lacking at present is a bookmark clustering device – we have as yet no collective noun for a collection of useful web pages and to share your favourite websites you still need to sit down and build a page with the links – not the most straightforward of tasks.

Filling the learning pot

The greatest enemy of promise for many learners is the blank sheet of A4, accompanied by a task along the lines of 'tell us what you know about.' Similarly, a computer screen showing a blank word-processing page can be just as intimidating a starting point for some learners. We know at times that poetry and works of art have happened when a genius met a blank page or an empty canvas, but before we can become geniuses we need suitable starting points and scaffolding for our learning.

Similarly, the solitary worksheet that the teacher managed to photocopy before the start of the lesson might soon be seen as an inadequate source of support and inspiration. New tools allow us to move easily beyond this model, beyond the blank page and the empty information store – the learning pot need never be empty again. ICT, creatively deployed, and fed by a large online corpus of resources, can support and scaffold rich learning journeys. Where there is learner choice there is a higher level of brain engagement than when tasked with simply a comprehension exercise. With multiple sources, evaluation must be exercised, comparisons can be made, ideas contrasted, variation explored, with the learner, at times, able to play to their strengths and preferences.

With internet access for the classroom there need not always be just a single resource such as a poem, picture or sound, for two resources provides the means for comparison and contrast, and this process often provides the pivot for dialogue and engagement. The notion of 'binary opposition' is a key principle in designing positive learning activities and this approach is now fed by the wealth of resources provided by the internet. In the internet age a page of solid text will begin to look like a curious mono-media learning resource. For visual cues are an easy addition to any document, retrieved using Google's image search engine, or captured from the real world with a digital camera. Every picture tells a story and visual resources offer a cognitive extension to broaden the power of expression.

Binary opposition in action

Compare these features – What's the same? What's different?

Tapping into a larger brain

 There was a second part of the dream, too, dependent on the web being so generally used that it became a realistic mirror (or in fact the primary embodiment) of the ways in which we work and play and socialize. That was that once the state of our interactions was online, we could then use computers to help us analyze it, make sense of what we are doing, where we individually fit in, and how we can better work together.

Tim Berners-Lee (1998)

WEBSITE

For many knowledge workers, the internet is now a constant companion. It flicks new emails into their line of sight as they work on other documents. It tempts them to dive into an internet search at moments when they can't quite think of the right term or reference, and, mid-word, sudden doubt about spelling leads to a quick typing of www.dictionary.com into the browser in order to reassure. The above quote by Tim Berners-Lee reflects on the possibility that the internet could play a much larger part in our lives in not only helping us to spell, but also in making sense of many more of our individual actions, our doubts and our aspirations.

Although the internet is destined to increasingly underpin our professional and social lives, its greatest potential perhaps lies in its communication rather than information role. Maybe the real power of the internet will be shown to lie, not in vast online libraries, but in the more simple human interconnections promoted through the exchange of experience in emails and user groups.

Teachers are starting to examine the possibilities of the internet for professional dialogue. A start has been made with Talking Heads, a private, virtual community supporting headteachers. The key success factor in the collaborative environment that Talking Heads illustrates is the importance of human dimension provided by mentors online. The experienced mentors nurse new arrivals through their first virtual experiences, encouraging headteachers to use the tools of the system to make suggestions and to participate in adding thoughts to bulletin boards.

Similarly, if you were a special needs teacher in a remote school then subscribing to a user group of similar professionals could provide a powerful and engaging means of professional support and interaction albeit at a distance. Once subscribed, the ebb and flow of questions between teachers will appear on screen or via email reflecting a professional exchange of ideas and experiences. This also overcomes the passive trap of expert material lying out there undiscovered – the distillation of a shared experience often provides a fast track through real and virtual resource banks, and guides new recruits to the professional gold nuggets that lie in cyberspace.

Tapping into a bigger and connected brain

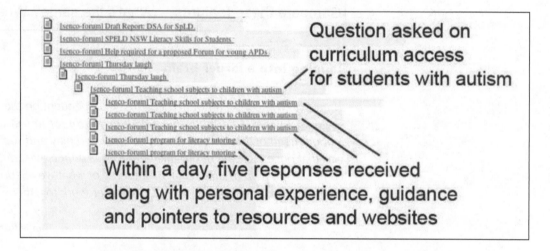

Sharing the learning recipe

I once listened to two teachers arguing: 'We can't put that on the wall,' said one, 'or the students will know what they have to do.' The constraints of some syllabuses make this scenario common at times. If you don't know the right answer or desired end result that is expected it's hard to be a brave and fearless learner. Examples of what learning performance looks like at various ages and levels are like gold dust – and like gold dust they are rare.

So what does learning/performance look like? An example of a website that manages to provide some answers is the National Curriculum in Action site (www.ncaction.org.uk). This website, one of the most useful resources ever to emerge from a government department, is dedicated to providing real examples of students' work, and case study material to show what the national curriculum looks like in practice. It's all here from art to ICT by way of music at all Key Stages and most attainment levels. Written work is scanned in so you

WEBSITE

can even see the child's real handwriting. Music is recorded and is available as a sound file. This means that it's even possible to download and listen to a piece of jazz improvisation at KS3, level 4.

Home page of National Curriculum in Action website (reproduced by permission of QCA)

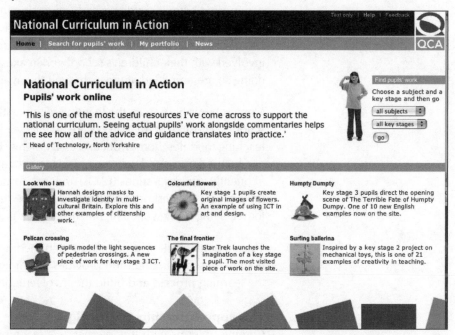

At a recent training event, student teachers mapped their experience against examples taken straight from the site for their subjects and age group. 'I wanted to show my students what a level 3 piece of history work should look like and now I can', said a history trainee. A science graduate trainee noted, 'It's such a relief to use the site to find out that my students' work matches what's going on in other classrooms – it's good to see that our expectations correlate with reality.'

With a little guidance and mediation, the site contents are useful for students as they can see dispassionately how they measure up and can see the standard they should realistically be aiming for. As well as examples of work, there are materials detailing the process students go through as they carry out this work. So a discussion about light and dark between two students is available as a video clip on the site. Extra resources allow each example to be converted into a lesson plan and you can also save your own portfolio of evidence as an online index of favourite examples.

WEBSITE

> **Taking it further**
> Some schools turn the internet into a treasure hunt. First make up a worksheet listing three websites and build an activity around a treasure hunt idea so that students find and piece together information from each site – a bit like a detective game. In the US, they call lessons designed in this way WebQuests (log onto http://webquest.sdsu.edu). There are hundreds of web lessons here, including a lovely lesson for Reception class on the *World of Puppets*, which takes children to Japan, Vietnam and Bali as they investigate the local cultural use of puppetry and figures.

Getting parents involved

What are the benefits of educating parents as well as children? The benefits may well be greater than we might think at first. A recent piece of research from the UK government has shown that young children whose parents were directly involved in their learning had better language skills and were more numerate than those whose parents took a less active part. Children whose parents participated in their children's early education through the Peers Early Education Partnership (PEEP) achieved systematically five percentage points more in language comprehension than those who didn't. Getting parents actively involved with their children's schoolwork makes sense, and the opportunities for doing so are amplified at times through the availability of the internet.

Many schools now share the learning recipe with parents on a public part of the school's website. There, parents are able to see learning overviews, maps of the teaching modules, homework and assignments. Email and text to mobile phones can be used as a rapid way for parents to get answers to a question. Answers to frequently asked questions (FAQs) and web forums could also provide scope for parents to ask questions anonymously. Some teachers now make use of email for receiving homework assignments and for giving feedback between lessons.

The school website is a potentially rich medium for communications between home and school. Email too provides an immediacy of response that can aid the learning process and build the involvement of parents.

The apprenticeship of the digital age

Coming to terms with the internet as a teaching tool also requires teachers to help students move beyond digital plagiarism – where students copy and paste information from another source and pass it off as their own. Strategies to counter this process need to be taught in schools. One delightful strategy devised by a headteacher involves returning suspect work to students with every seventh word deleted making the student fill in the gaps in their 'own' work. Tools like Hot Potatoes (www.halfbaked.com) can be used to generate these cloze procedures on any text.

WEBSITE

Locking in the learning by hitting the media shift key

WEBSITE

Feeding yourself on the internet

Visit a search engine – a place on the internet that keeps a record of the content of most web pages – my current favourite is Google (www.google.com). Then type in 'getting started in PowerPoint' or the subject or software of interest to you, such as 'animation.'

The first ten to 20 matches will come from web addresses culminating in '.edu' (American Universities) or from those labelled '.ac' (UK universities), meaning that they are likely to be professional, accurate and available for use in the public domain – subject to any listed site restrictions. In addition, you have tapped into the combined resources of hundreds of universities.

Bad web pages in terms of poor design or inappropriate, scurrilous or evil materials can become good teaching resources. Teachers need to explicitly use them and annotate why they are poor/dangerous/pointless sites for research. Such exemplification would be an ideal subject for a whole-year lecture in the turbo-teaching zone perhaps (see Chapter 5).

We live at a time when we have mislaid the concept of apprenticeship. At a time when our tools are more powerful and far-reaching than any age, we have stopped many of the processes that have helped us pass on models of productive use so efficiently in the past. The best use of tools occurs when students are taught their operation over time with the resultant attempts at individual use mediated and commented on as a group learning experience. 'Harry, let's look at the history folder in your web browser which shows us how you carried out this research – talk us through what choices you made about pages you looked at and why.'

Take us back through the process that got you to here

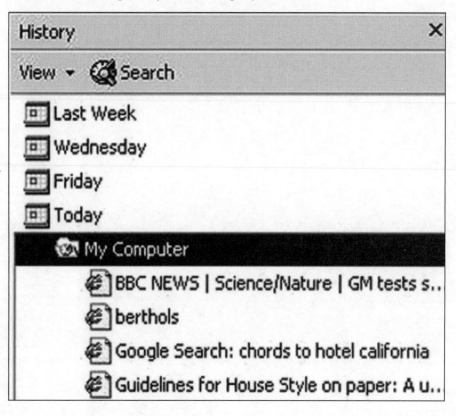

Chapter 5

Building new learning environments

▌Opportunities and pitfalls in ICT integration

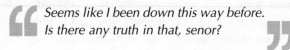

> *Seems like I been down this way before.*
> *Is there any truth in that, senor?*

'Senor-Tales of Yankee Power', Bob Dylan

Around 30 years ago beauty came to our schools – especially at the primary level. Bright colours, instructive displays and tactile learning opportunities were the order of the day – all learning needs and styles were met almost intuitively by teachers working in an appropriate environment with a fair amount of professional freedom. Then came the computer. We built rooms around them without much regard for learning styles, needs or differences. In fact, as the computer made its first forced march into classrooms, educators were strangely silent about making it fit the mould of existing good practice.

This was a new technology, it came with its own relentless momentum – students were clearly motivated and that as far as it went. 'Motivation pure and simple' was to be the justification for this drive. Now, various governments in the UK and the US are busy trying to retrospectively map some greater cognitive plan onto the early days of computers in schools – trying in part to explain why we spent so much, so quickly, for no observable gain in the quality or quantity of learning. This is likely to prove to be a fruitless exercise though and the best we can really say is that we did some serious shopping back then when technology was expensive. We can still learn from this experience however and use it to inform future developments.

Education development is littered with the detritus of technology-led initiatives. We could begin to make things better for the future if we map what we know about learning onto the tools we have available today, and learn to deploy them appropriately within the learning environment.

Recent attempts have been made to prove a causal link between ICT investment and exam success in the UK and indeed some research has shown a tentative link – schools using ICT well tend to have good results in English, maths and science – but one might turn this logic around and say that a school getting good results generally could also be expected to get ICT integration right as well.

Similarly, statistical comparisons show that a high level of ICT use improves GCSE results in modern foreign languages and in science by a proportion of a GCSE grade. The real question, however, is if we wanted to improve results in these subjects, could we have done a more direct job with a smaller sum of money than it has cost to fill schools with computers with little regard to qualitative issues? This is not to deny the fact the computer is potentially the most effective teaching and learning resource yet invented. It is simply that its journey into the history of teaching practice has paid insufficient attention to its impact on learning.

In the last 20 years, many learning environments built with the computer in mind have become a little more barren in terms of the needs of learners and the learning diet less varied. When computers were first used in school, slide shows, film shows, epidiascopes and spirit duplicated school newsletters had disappeared, and it seemed at times as if the diet had narrowed to just having one's turn on a computer. Far from extending the range of the learning experience the use of the computer had at times served to narrow it down to 'text on screen served cold'. Instead of enriching the learning experience, ICT has at times served to downgrade it. But slowly the potential of the tools was recognized, as was the scaffolding they provide to allow us to tap into motivational learning opportunities. We know there is gold buried here – it's just taking longer than expected to find it.

Environment matters – maybe even more than we think
Henry Morris, Secretary of Education for Cambridgeshire, 1922-1954, saw the buildings, landscape and public works of art we encounter in our daily round as powerful, inspiring and educative environments in their own right.

The design, decoration and equipment of our places of education cannot be regarded as anything less than of first-rate importance – as equally important, indeed, as the teacher.

Morris (1930s), speech at the opening of
Impington Village College, Cambridgshire

Too much office, too little supermarket

The history of ICT in the school environment could be characterized as 'too much office, too little supermarket'. Our learning from the office – which had learned from the typing pool, and thence the factory – has been quite relentless. Offices had desks with rows of computers and schools quickly followed suit (or should that be suite). Offices had nice springy chairs with four, then five wheels, and schools kept up with the pace not noticing that the purpose of schools is entirely different to that of the office.

Offices are also about productivity – usually this means using workforce and tools in the most efficient way to maximize profits. Schools are places concerned with the education and training of young people to be knowledgeable, skilled, capable, adaptable, qualified and with the attributes necessary to continue to learn and drive their own careers forward. The uses of ICT should mirror those key purposes of schools in the way that they are used. ICT needs to be used creatively for promoting research and thinking skills, for developing understanding through enquiry, for learning how to learn and to develop an all-round capability as a lifelong learner.

Schools are about diversity and, at times, awkward enquiry, argument and understanding, all mixed in a heady brew of dialogue and the written word. The orderly, consistent and homogeneous world of the office system provides an ill fitting format for the process of learning in many classrooms. Schools are not offices and it's time to move beyond any mindsets that would seek to make them so.

Ironically though, the concept of the workstation (rather than the office) is finding its way into the ICT practice of some US schools with very positive results, as reported by Alan November (2004). Students in these schools spend half the day in classrooms being taught, and half the day in a workstation environment working on personal assignments (aided by a tutor). Here they have the freedom to think and work for themselves applying the skills they have been taught. They can exercise choice over how they choose to work, and they have the resources to aid these choices. In this sense, they have the choice of the supermarket combined with the practices of the modern knowledge worker.

Schools of the future will probably abandon the model of the old style office and typing pool, in favour of methods that promote more effectively the aims of the school and the abilities of the learner. Some may look at the separate notions of effective teaching and effective learning and provide time when each is allowed to occur in its most effective and separate way. It is unlikely that we will still promote the idea of a homogeneous 'lesson' in the school of the future, recurring throughout the day in one-hour slots punctuated by bells. A more blended set of learning opportunities are more likely to be the norm.

Learning from a wider world

Now is a good time to cast our net of inspiration a little wider and to learn from other integrations of technology in the workplace. To return to the supermarket, for example, when was the last time we saw someone struggle with a mouse and keyboard at the checkout or the petrol station till? Here, slimline touch screens are prevalent – allowing space for face to face communication, and returning users to the ultimate and original pointing device of the human finger.

Supermarkets have even trained us to use touch screens, to select vouchers on entry to the store and bar-code readers to process our own shopping – perhaps school libraries could manage to provide the same technologies to support browsing internet users in the same way at lunchtimes. It's time for schools to trust themselves, to glean ideas on the creative use of new tools from wherever they see fit.

Keeping a level head

When the current wave of education change and technology development across the world has settled down and bedded in, we will probably find that the answers to the future were safely nested all along in the experiences of the past.

The debate in 2005 about the relative value of interactive whiteboards and projectors will possibly be seen as insignificant when placed against ambitious plans to build new schools for the future that could really use ICT to make a significant difference. The creation of larger teaching zones for multimedia lectures and exemplification by staff and students would be an option for exploiting the power of ICT with fewer constraints, than currently trying to use it in classrooms that were never designed with ICT in mind.

Without reflection, action research and the sharing of experience, interactive whiteboards might be seen to yield to tablet PCs, which in turn could yield to the next new thing. As had been the case for some years, nobody benefits in a headlong dash towards the newest technology except the manufacturers.

Governments and teachers alike could follow the advice not to put their shirt on any one technology. Instead, a sensible focus will be on how the deployment and management of a variety of technological and software tools can improve pedagogy and learning opportunities.

At times, we might find we can learn more from the structures and strategies of the medieval monastery than from the modern office. Indeed, there might be some point to the argument that there were more multisensory learning opportunities present in a fifteenth-century church than in a typical classroom in the twenty first-century. Here we would find music, plainchant, large vivid illustrations on the lives of saints and bible stories, opportunities for bodily movement and prayer beads for the congregation to indulge their visual, auditory, tactile and kinesthetic needs while worshipping. Books would contain illuminated type with a single memorable picture leading those who could read into the text, or providing a visual clue to understanding to those who were simply looking on in awe.

In monasteries, monks often stood to work, write, draw and access their visual field by looking upwards at high windows and wall illustrations. Many Victorian classrooms mimicked this approach. Until the last century, most writers and bookkeepers worked standing up at a high lectern desk or sitting on a high stool. Many of today's learners have a learning style preference for standing, or sitting at a higher level – a need not met in the 'one size fits all' approach to office furnishing. Since medieval times, people have delighted in and recognized the power of music, song and chant, the use of natural light, writing slopes and illuminated scripts – the list is long and can serve to inform the learning environments we now aspire to build in order to transform the learning potential of tomorrow's learners.

Always more than one way of doing things

'THINKING BEYOND THE OFFICE - STANDING, THE NEW SITTING?'

Now consider the office of the late twentieth century, with its desks and photocopiers and word processors as far as the eye can see, with hunched-over workers looking downwards into laptops as they work. Here we may see ourselves going back to the future as many new schools turn their backs on office design to mimic the monasteries of old with space, south-facing windows and natural light. A poor environment with computers is precisely that – a poor environment for learning.

Time for a broader view

The ubiquitous computer with its typical three-part structure – monitor, processor box and keyboard – is the enduring generic symbol of ICT. But computers, thus portrayed, may not be the best single blueprint for providing the ultimate learning experience. The narrow focus which education has taken on the computer, particularly in its buying habits, has probably had a narrowing effect on our imagination in developing learning with ICT. If this persists, it may lead to the exclusion of many sleeker, more immediately useful technologies that might arrive at our classroom doors. The mobile phone is a good example of an emergent technology – first banned by headteachers – it now has huge potential as a communication aid for learning and assessment.

Planning for portability

Mobile devices such as phones, MP3 players and small personal digital assistants (PDAs) are likely to prove to be significant technologies for future learning tools. What the brave future gazer would not have guessed five years ago is the current level of mobile phone ownership among school children – many at that time were speaking mistakenly of a laptop in every satchel – a vision that still looks like being some way off. Search for the smallest and the neatest technology and you will normally have a fairly good glimpse of the future.

It is the fact that such technologies are both small and portable that is the key to their adoption, in the sense that they are truly personal devices in the way that a laptop is not, or at least not yet. Keyboard size determines the less than ergonomic size of the laptop, making it a less than convenient accoutrement for the modern young person while battery life (improving, but still relatively unimpressive) also means that one doesn't venture very far from an electrical plug.

A recent pilot project, eVIVA, developed by the team at Ultralab Research Lab in Chelmsford, England, tapped into the possibilities of mobile technologies by allowing students (aged 14) to display their competence in using ICT by calling a free phone number and talking through their understanding of a number of ICT skills in response to some pre-recorded questions. The students' recorded voices were then automatically digitized and placed on a website for their teachers to listen to and accredit at a time of their choosing.

Case study

eViva project

After registering with the project website, students build a portfolio by sending examples of work with annotations. They eventually choose five questions that they work towards answering as part of a telephone viva (oral test of knowledge).

As they work, the students post milestones of annotated work on the website. A text-messaging facility is also built into the site so that students can send text messages of ideas and reflections straight to their portfolio online. When students feel ready for their viva, they phone a free phone number where they answer the questions prompted by a pre-recorded voice. Answers can be re-recorded if the students wish and the final versions are stored as sound files in their area on the site, accessible only to students and their teachers. Calls are free from Orange who are providing network support for the pilot.

The system is also about to go into use in New Zealand. Several examination boards in the UK are exploring the potential of the model. Professor Stephen Heppell, Director of Ultralab, sees small portable devices like the latest generation mobile phones as key technologies for future learning.

At a recent conference, Heppell handed out a number of mobile phones to headteachers and asked them to text their thoughts straight from their phones to a web page he was displaying live on screen – 'The response was incredible,' says Heppell, 'it's so immediate, you send text and it's there.' He now gives out a number at the start of his presentations and his audience can text what they think about his presentation as it proceeds – the responses appearing in a small window on his presentation screen. Imagine that as a tool in the classroom, where teachers get direct feedback from their pupils as the lesson progresses.

The power of projection

One key development for the classroom teacher has been the video/data projector which arrived in school in the mid-1990s. This device proved a breakthrough resource as technology now came to the front of the class and was mediated by the teacher. New opportunities arose to broaden the bandwidth of classroom teaching with different learning styles in mind. Unlike a blackboard, where all that was to be seen had to be created by the teacher's hand and stick of chalk, the data projector could display a range of textual and visual imagery, both still and moving, contained within a PowerPoint presentation. Over time, the teacher could build up a large bank of such slides and assemble them rapidly to match the subject of the lesson. The ability to 'draw' over a slide provided the teacher with a familiar ability to jot, to highlight, to draw attention and to erase. Enhancing that first learning medium – stick marks in the sand – the interactive whiteboard brings interactivity to the locus of communication between teacher and learner.

With the arrival of the data projector things changed. The pendulum began to swing away from providing specialist rooms for ICT access towards taking these new tools to the front of the classroom for the teacher to introduce and mediate, and for students to demonstrate their understanding.

Time to project ourselves

Projectors have now become increasingly bright and quiet – two key points for those considering purchase. Many schools have taken the next step and added an interactive whiteboard to combine with the projected image. For many teachers, the use of these devices connected to the internet has allowed them to explore the blending of a variety of media in their teaching. It has also provided a subtle way of encouraging a broadening of teaching styles and approaches. The scaffolding effect of the technology allows teachers to experiment outside the comfort zone of 'chalk and talk'.

Using the computer and a projector to get the most out of assemblies

Idea 1

Try using PowerPoint and the 'Rehearse Timings' option under 'Slide Show' on the main menu. This allows you to synchronize your display so that it changes in time to a piece of music, or soundtrack of your choice. You could use it to display some pictures and thoughts about recent work as children enter the hall.

Idea 2

At the end of an assembly you can use a wheel mouse (an inexpensive mouse with a wheel in its centre) to automatically scroll down a diary of the week ahead that has been saved in Word or as a web page. Either of these uses will be enhanced by the selection of a suitable piece of Mozart or equivalent played through the computer or any other sound system.

Wheel mouse – the reinvented wheel

In recent times, the interactive whiteboard marched into most schools across the UK as a 'must have' piece of new technology. After a period of exploration, guidance on best practice began to emerge and be shared. The LISA (literacy in subject areas) project in Islington, London, was set up to learn and share some of the lessons learned from classroom use of these new tools. 'It's all about going beyond display,' says Linda Dawson, project leader with the North Islington education action zone (EAZ) – a government funded education initiative who sponsor the work. 'We are convinced that the way forward is enhancing classroom talk and discourse through the use of this tool. One of the dangers of the whiteboard is that it is a lovely presentation tool but if we only use it for presentation it could become like "pretty wallpaper" – and we could lose an opportunity for promoting some effective classroom interaction.'

Alongside the many examples of inclusive and stimulating use of the interactive whiteboard, there will probably be cases of classroom ennui brought about by overuse of a single technology for relentless visual display – 'just for the sake of it', 'because it was there' or 'the head said I had to'.

This is again a consequence of the enduring assumption that ICT will always be 'motivating' and a possible lack of thought about how learning can be made more effective by the choices made about how an item of technology is used. The integration of whiteboards and other new devices into the learning process will be a developmental and dynamic issue for schools. Choices over how ICT is used will need to be checked against its effect on the learning of individuals. It is another example of where one size is unlikely to fit all.

Hitting the passive/active switch

When reviewing the impact of technology in the classroom it helps to examine the active/passive balance. A general principle is that, at the most elemental level, learning arises from doing. In many cases, the learner is likely to benefit more from a practical engagement with the subject being taught than with the passive reception of visuals and talk, however pyrotechnic, from the front of the class.

Physiology, ergonomics and delightful learning environments

ergonomics – *the applied science of equipment design, as for the workplace, intended to maximize productivity by reducing operator fatigue and discomfort.*

Will *Homo sapiens* reassert their upright posture or will the laptop crunch continue?

One body – many ways of working with technology:
- ➡ *Homo* laptopus – *face down crouched over machine*
- ➡ *standing up at lectern with laptop*
- ➡ *cuddled up with a tablet.*

Ergonomy, the study of human–machine interaction, becomes increasingly important as schools move to increasing laptop provision, wireless networks, and the use of small portable devices in class. We will need new models of good practice and ideas on how to integrate these tools in classrooms in delightful and creative ways that will make a difference for learners. Any designed environment should ideally be fit for purpose, cost-effective and a delight to the eye. Taking this design rubric as an obvious starting point, it is hard to see why, in the past, we have presided over so many computer environments which are badly laid out, expensive and generally unappealing.

It is still possible, and occasionally the norm, for some schools and colleges to spend anything up to one million pounds on ICT provision, and yet, along the way, only talk to computer sales people. Teachers and learners are often excluded from such discussions. The result is that we often shoehorn yet more computers into schools with little concern for purposeful use or good design. If governments focus on computer-to-pupil ratios rather than indicators of effective use it makes the numbers game even more compelling for schools to play.

If rooms get filled with large boxes and screens, multi-purpose learning opportunities are in turn banished in favour of individual screen gazing. It remains important to put the learning environment first and sculpt the use of ICT to meet the learners' needs. It is also time for schools and teaching staff to take charge and have a major input into classroom design and the integration of software and hardware tools for learning.

WEBSITE

Research from The Helen Hamlyn Research Centre (www.hhrc.rca.ac.uk), at the Royal College of Art, has reported that teachers' views are not adequately represented in the commission and design of new school facilities and equipment.

One school parent will often spend more on a kitchen redesign and ergonomic study, than a school with over 1,500 pupils will have spent considering the learning environment and how new (and old) tools for learning can best be integrated.

Case study

Organic learning areas

Powerful transformations are possible when teachers take control of designing their own learning environments. Vivi Lachs of the Highwire Learning Centre in Hackney, London, UK, recounts what steps they took in developing their City Learning Centre: 'The way we design spaces reflects a philosophy of learning. At Highwire it is the learning, not the computers, that are central. We want students to engage with ideas and use the technology, rather than simply engaging with the technology. We want them to collaborate in group-work.'

Organic curves, PODs and zoning

'At Highwire, there are no rows that serve to make the computer the focus. We have tried to create adaptable spaces where computers are hidden and built into the structure, so that students can choose when it is appropriate to use them, and have space for any other work as well. Local carpenters were employed by the centre to build bespoke computer desks and flat computer screens were built into the desk lids.'

Homo laptopus **and telesales – a cautionary tale**

The next time someone tries to sell you life assurance, or something similar on the telephone, ask them if they are standing up or sitting down. Chances are they will be standing up, moving about accessing their visual field, possibly juggling three balls in the air and anticipating all your objections before you even make them. You on the other hand may be sitting at a desk, eyes down in your feelings zone as you work on your laptop. There is an unequal competition at play here.

It is often the same in the classroom. The teacher – the one with the degree – asks the questions. The teacher is the only one standing up, taking in oxygen and 'seeing the possibilities' – in full control in fact. The design of ICT in the learning environment should allow for a variety of learning style needs – along with a place to draw, read, write, record sound and edit images.

As a general principle, we should design learning environments with making, saying and showing in mind. Opportunities for story-telling and narrative should be fostered across a variety of media, with a local audience in mind. Are there places to perform, sit and listen, places to sculpt, edit and publish, using sound, pictures and text? Are there places where students can stand, sit to use a laptop or perch at a high stool and write?

Decisions about whether to stand or sit also includes hardness of seat, position of the screen and mouse and screen brightness. These are areas over which students could be given some options, alternatives and control. If variations of this sort are present then students can self-select, partly governed by their individual preferences.

Many restaurants allow self-selection opportunities for customers without a word being spoken, simply by lighting one side of a table more than the other and allowing customers to choose their preferred side. Could the same approach work in the classroom?

The key, believes Mark Champkins, a designer specializing in the needs of the learner in the classroom, is to engage the requirements of the teachers more directly in the design process to tackle problems in both new build and existing classrooms.

WEBSITE

To illustrate potential areas for development, Champkins has developed a suite of five conceptual design proposals to enhance concentration (http://www.concentrate.org.uk). A water bottle which doubles as a pencil holder encouraging pupils to drink sufficiently in lessons. A school bag lives a separate life as a backrest when fitted over the chair back, making the chair more comfortable.

Are you sitting comfortably?

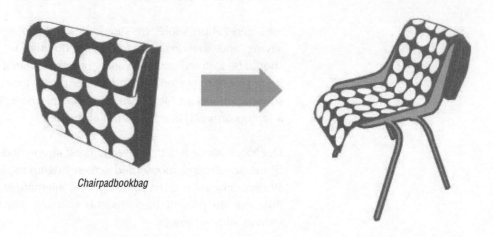

Chairpadbookbag

Like the padded book bag, a new material called Stomatex was used to form the cushion. This fabric allows the skin to breathe, stopping the seat from becoming sweaty.

Knowledge transfer works

We can often learn from another iteration of successful 'teachnology' integration in an area of experience very different from our own and benefit from their accumulated wisdom. Some use the term 'benchmarking' for the process of taking an idea that worked well in one sector and using it in another. What makes a café successful? What aspects of the experience can we bring to the school's 'learning centre' or whatever we are calling the school library this week.

Organic planning

Organic planning could be the term used to describe a process of development that can adapt to the responses and successes of the individuals affected by it. Organic planning can be achieved by starting with the broad-brush precepts and then specifying the underlying principles that will serve to guide our decisions. As the plan moves forward, it evolves to maintain the best level of customer satisfaction – in this case the experiences and reflected views of learners and teachers. Compare this to casting a single approach in stone for the next five years by building a plan around the perceived rules and constraints of a technology that will certainly be out of date before the ultimate learning goals are achieved.

Starter set of provisions to consider in environment development:

➡ Light/shade/glare reduction on projection surfaces

➡ Colour of floor/walls/transient adaptation

➡ Portable/fixed/large/small

➡ Sitting/standing

➡ Sound/silence

➡ Collaborative space

➡ Large group zones

➡ Textures

➡ Eye line.

Case study

David Turrell, headteacher of Sir Bernard Lovell School in Bristol, UK says; 'Our priorities are teaching and learning. We are using ICT as a major tool in the process but it's absolutely critical that the whole environment looks right – and computers are only part of the overall equation. With this approach the school has just completed a new design building constructed on an open plan basis for 180 students with 60 computers. It's a multipurpose area that supports whole-class, team teaching and individual work.'

It is time to look beyond the assembled ranks of box-shifting PC companies, regardless of their lineage. Teachers need support as they look to a new horizon where teaching and learning are the objectives, and ICT-rich learning environments are developed with delight, engagement and dialogue in mind, rather than megabytes.

Large, room dominating and exclusively computer-focused approaches to ICT are fast becoming the dinosaurs of the digital age. The classroom of the future is a concept to be reinvented by each individual teacher.

In schools, wireless connected laptops are now becoming commonplace, and large bulky grey computer monitors are being pushed out by svelte LCD screens. Projectors and tablet devices will proliferate, linked via the airwaves as wires disappear. It seems that technology is now starting to make learning environments beautiful after having made them ugly for so long. Some companies, such as Sony and Apple, have long understood the need for devices that delight by form as well as function, and that message will be welcomed by every school building their own unique and delightful variation on the classroom of the future.

Students and teachers will over time tap into the digital catalysis – a medium that delights and encourages further immersion – using tools that are powerful for learning, culturally cool, intrinsically portable and practically personal.

If you doubt this prediction, let me invite you to cast your mind's eye back to that first stuffy computer room that heralded a revolution in education that is still to come. Now let us compare that to the best integrated use of ICT that has been reported in recent times.

Change the physiology – change the state

Imagine for a moment you are at the door greeting a class at the start of a lesson. Run the imagined event further. Bring them into the room and start teaching. Now become aware of your arms. What are they doing? Are they neatly by your side or have they started to rise and point upwards? If they have it's because you are intuitively encouraging children to move out of the domain of their feelings (often externally indicated by students looking downwards) and up into their visual field to take in information from you and your chosen display media and to imagine described events. An old maxim in accelerated learning is that to change a learner's state you often have to change the way in which they are standing or sitting, looking and breathing. Change the physiology – change the state. In other words, the daily effort to get students out of their feelings and up into their visual field is supported by research. We look down to access our emotions and we look up to see and visualize what might be.

Eye movements as a clue to sensory processing

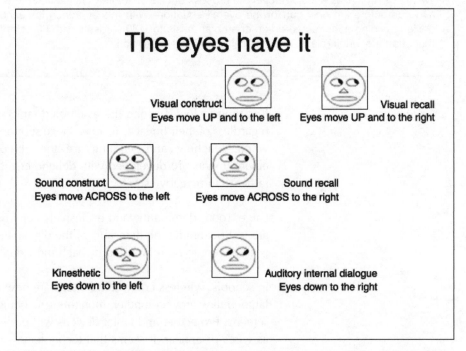

The eyes have it

Visual construct
Eyes move UP and to the left

Visual recall
Eyes move UP and to the right

Sound construct
Eyes move ACROSS to the left

Sound recall
Eyes move ACROSS to the right

Kinesthetic
Eyes down to the left

Auditory internal dialogue
Eyes down to the right

Research into eye movements as an indicator of internal sensory and cognitive processing activity has created a matrix of eye movements in various quadrants.

To make the most of this knowledge, we need to consider the posture which is adopted when we use different types of ICT. Many computer monitors, and especially laptops, can lead to a head down, classic collapsed chest posture with the user looking downwards and into their feelings and where oxygen intake is limited because the thoracic cavity is closed inwards.

In this position, it may well be physically more difficult for the learner to visualize, see opportunities or consider alternatives. Try this for yourself. Sit at a desk and imagine you have a laptop if front of you on which you are typing – look downwards to your hands as you type and adopt the classic pose of *Homo laptopus*. Now as you do so, imagine two alternative solutions to developing world debt – take 30 seconds and note down your answer. Now stand up and take three deep, slow breaths. Focus on a point slightly higher than eye level on a wall or in the distance. Imagine a place you know something of in the developing world and then answer the question again. Did you notice a difference? Some ergonomists consider sitting to be the worst thing for young learners. We need to remember that sitting is not a natural state for mankind as a species – even in well designed, comfortable chairs.

Standing – the new sitting?

It is more than likely that we will find standing to be the new sitting. Many children may prefer to stand to read or even to use a laptop. We can often see groups of pupils standing around a computer. They will move to respond to the activity on screen. Little hops of delight will accompany moments of success. Discussion and interplay happen naturally as group understanding and knowledge is built up. Such a stance – the group standing close together with a common focus – is a natural assembly of learners. A group sat down and separated is less natural.

Research suggests standing has less impact on the spine than sitting – perhaps we should be investigating more opportunities to provide standing access to books and computer screens in our classrooms. The digital lectern could live again as a viable alternative to the five-castor chair, so beloved of ICT suites the world over. Perhaps sitting is more about control than an attempt to find the optimum posture for learning.

The human frame it seems is not designed to sit at 90 degrees in a chair at a desk for long periods. Saddle type chairs are often considered the most effective for postural benefits, as you have to bring muscles into play to remain upright, and they serve to open up the chest and abdomen so breathing is freer and arm, hand and eye co-ordination are made easier.

The end of mouse dominance?

In years to come, we will look back on these mouse years as if they were some kind of spatial challenge activity that went on a bit too long. As if you were asked to read while juggling, or tap dance while you eat. In some ways, the mouse allows learners to move and touch – but in a highly structured and spatially challenging, limited way. Most of us are still struggling with the mouse while supermarkets and gas station cashiers luxuriate in the delight of the touch screen.

Once again, it's back to the future – with the tablet PC now reintegrating the movement of the hands, rather than working in another plane to the action on screen. For some teachers and learners, the spatial challenge of the mouse has made interaction and progress too laboured an activity for the time-pressed crucible of the classroom.

Lighting the way

Light, colour and sound are the three low cost ways of improving an environment, confirming a purpose and encouraging a positive state in the human mind.

The level of brightness in the learning environment is considered by many observers as a discrete part of an individual's environmental learning style and an area in which there will be considerable differences between learners. Many parents spend time at home switching on lights for their offspring to learn better, only for them to be switched off again because some learners prefer less light. In addition to environmental lighting, the level of screen brightness is another often forgotten variable. It is a bit like the choice of the position of the mouse and left or right hand preference, over which learners can easily be given some control.

Many teachers have noted the empirical evidence on how different lighting affects students' behaviour, alertness and ability to learn, as well as the way in which lighting affects their own performance.

Brise-soleil

The blending of natural and artificial light in the classroom is a secret weapon in the armoury of school improvement. Room lighting may not sound important but light has a direct effect on mood, which at its extremes gives rise to a winter condition called SAD, or seasonally affective disorder, which is curable by exposure to a strong source of light with similar characteristics to daylight.

It is likely that the best lighting for a classroom will be natural daylight. Some new school buildings are utilizing this once more and using brise-soleil (to diffuse direct rays of sunlight).

A teacher developing a classroom specifically linked to a range of learning style needs was asked what was the first thing she would to do to improve a learning environment. She replied, 'If you just want to do one thing which will have an immediate beneficial effect on learning – turn off the lights.'

The key issues here are visual comfort and providing appropriate light levels for all the various tasks and activities that take place in the classroom. The good news is that you don't have to break the budget to address both of these issues.

Use muslin and other materials below areas of high glare lighting to reduce the direct light

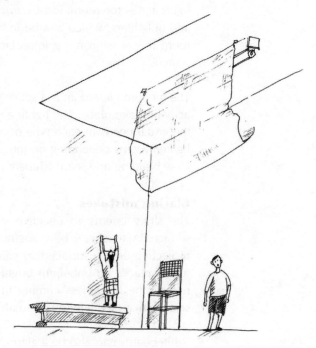

Individual preferences vary for light levels while learning, but glare is a distraction for all learners

Many specialists consider that the best approach to classroom lighting is a balance of indirect (up) light – light reflected from the ceiling that provides uniform ambient illumination throughout the space, and controlled direct (down) light, to provide enhanced visibility for reading and writing tasks. One aim should be to diffuse as much of the available light as possible to avoid serious shadows or glares from any given area. A key to balanced lighting is to avoid high levels of transient adaptation – as eyes move around a space they adapt to the brightness of various surfaces. If you look at a bright light source, or window, and the next instant look at a dark wall or carpet, the eyes must work hard to make the transition. Too much transient adaptation can lead to eye fatigue. Dark colour carpets, though serviceable in high volume of use, may not be the best choice, because dark colours generally absorb more light and require greater wattage to get the same degree of lighting as in a room painted in lighter shades.

Electronic ballasts get rid of much of the flicker and hum suffered by the earlier analogue versions, and save energy by reducing electrical losses in both the ballast and the lamps. Most computer displays have some flicker, and if you also have flicker in your lighting system it can cause tiredness and other detrimental effects on concentration. Newer LCD displays and those fitted to laptops also have less flicker than old style monitors.

Similarly, modern strip lights do not flicker as much as earlier tubes. However, many commentators have noted that the colour 'temperature' of the light is important. Artificial light has tended to be more yellow than daylight. Modern fluorescent tubes (called 'daylight bulbs') can get close to reproducing the range of frequencies that make up natural light. 'Warm white' is another option which produces a more 'sunny', yellowy effect, but is probably not quite as good a choice.

The best overhead lighting for classrooms should be shielded to project vertically downwards, so students will not be bothered by the direct glare from lights across the room. Ideally, down lights should be augmented by desk lamps and uplighters, which can be individually angled. If there are monitors in the room this is even more important as ordinary strip lights tend to reflect off screens.

The modern classroom is a space where a wide range of teaching and learning activities take place. The lighting needs to provide the flexibility in response to the visual needs of each type of activity. To this end, the ability to brighten or lighten rooms depending on the activity is something that should be planned. New building and refurbishment projects should seek lighting design advice.

Glaring mistakes

The shiny enemy to effective visual communication is the plastic coated surface. A teacher's best attempts to use simple multimedia, in this case projecting onto a surface that can also be written on, is often foiled by glare which places an unhelpful bright disc at the centre of their field of view, or reflects the brightness coming in through the windows. Similarly, computer screens that face windows can also give rise to 'IT room squint'.

Whiteboards can also be a glaring step backwards when used with a projector or OHP. In many classrooms, children will be forced to sit and watch the glare. It's often an unquestioned irritant for learners, which was never the case with blackboards.

The quality of communication in learning remains a priority. Think how you felt about a presentation that you could only see partially. It is part of the teacher's art to ensure they are communicating in the most effective way, and pupils' right to expect as much.

White A4 pages and strong overhead lighting compound the glare effect for many learners. It can be uncomfortable to read and can make concentration difficult. Covering the page with a transparent coloured plastic can help tone down the brightness as can using coloured paper. A technique used with dyslexic learners is to let them read text through a blue acetate sheet, which avoids the equivalent of 'snow blindness'. This is also a good tip for those who need to spend a lot of time reading documents.

There are strategies for tackling glare in the classroom. For example, using screens with a matt finish – there are some interactive whiteboard surfaces that can also be written on – and at times it's possible to use the 'pen' tool in PowerPoint instead. A white painted pinboard or similar matt surface is also better than a whiteboard to absorb the glare rather than reflect it.

Whatever visual tools deployed in the classroom, from poster to OHP to computer, through television to digital projector to whiteboard, students are likely to receive and retain more if images are shown up in the learners' visual field.

Zoning

Another key opportunity with ICT in the classroom environment is to gather and deploy resources according to their potential use as learning tools. Computers should be rated and labelled by their contribution to the learning outcome, not by their chip speed or popularity of the manufacturer. Zoning is part of the process involved in defining use by purpose. Zoning can help guide students towards work of particular cognitive challenge using selected modalities. The process can help to displace lower level activities such as aimless browsing or copy typing.

Creating activity zones in the classroom is a way to provide creative choice to pupils, particularly young learners

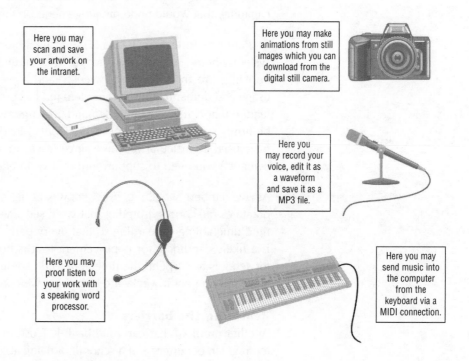

Here you may scan and save your artwork on the intranet.

Here you may make animations from still images which you can download from the digital still camera.

Here you may record your voice, edit it as a waveform and save it as a MP3 file.

Here you may proof listen to your work with a speaking word processor.

Here you may send music into the computer from the keyboard via a MIDI connection.

With zoning in mind, we can look afresh at the visual, auditory, kinesthetic and tactile aspects of the learning environment, both real and simulated, because at last we have some tools to help us manage their deployment. Classrooms could have a 'Show what you know zone' where students can at times put together short presentations of what they have understood. A scaled-down desk and smaller mouse can be made available for younger students, or a touch screen computer could be built into a podium with a projector hidden in the rostrum. One student can give the presentation and others can gather around offering sensitive feedback.

When planning the zones, we should ensure a range of tools are matched to learning modalities. Microphones, scanners and digital cameras are not luxuries but affordable tools which allow learners to work with a learning strength. It is surprising how readily schools with many computers already will use new money to buy more computers rather than additional peripherals that could make the existing fleet much more useful. Some schools go as far as illustrating the modalities at play with pictures on the wall, for example of 3D polystyrene hands and ears.

The use of zones can also be supported and managed by bookable access. We can link zoning in with record keeping on a bookable access basis, so that evidence of pupil's use of resources can be gathered. We could then use evidence on usage behaviours to support future developments and investment. There is good scope here too to provide evidence of the application of ICT capability that would underpin judgements on the ICT levels achieved by pupils.

At Palmers College in Grays, Essex, the library operates a simple booking system where students book access to computers in half hour time slots. The bookings are then processed weekly and a pie chart produced on levels of usage and demand. Times when demand has outstripped supply will point to a feature that is in substantial demand and arguments for further investment can be firmly supported by empirical evidence. Evidence that a thousand students have used a particular resource since it was made available is just the type of evidence you need to support further investment.

As we embed what we now know about learning effectiveness into the practices of schools, I predict that we'll see several changes taking place. The rigid timetabling of learning so that every part of the curriculum gets its share is a likely candidate for improvement -- it is becoming increasingly common for schools to suspend the timetable to do some different learning. No writing days and no pencil weeks are becoming welcome regular events.

Removing the barriers

Another problem that can hold back ICT use in schools is that bizarre, yet all too regular, occurrence of a school not being able to load a piece of software or download a file because they have insufficient access privileges. It might then require the teacher to adopt a begging position in front of the ICT co-ordinator, or worse still, a phone call to the town hall and a brush with corporate policy.

It is difficult for individual teachers or departments to develop brave and creative use beyond the applications of the office (word-processing and spreadsheets) when the focus of control is taken away from individuals and sometimes the school itself.

At times, development is thwarted when a teacher cannot install simple software or use a scanner locally without intervention from a 'network manager' who will generally be able to cite a dozen reasons why the request can't be agreed to. In many schools, the very real dangers of the internet gives rise to that major blocking word known as 'security'. It's even possible that some network managers will hide behind this term rather than find creative ways around problems. In consequence, many school ICT investments do not come to fruition as the scope of what pupils are able to do closes down to the safe common denominator and the run-of-the-mill ICT uses. School senior managers must avoid (where possible) being blinded by science in such cases and seek to press for the development of ambitious and enabling uses of ICT that give real value for money in terms of learning outcomes.

The large business model which has driven the management culture of ICT in schools suits schools less well than businesses, as schools need to cater for diverse needs, motivations and abilities, rather than homogeneous centralized provision.

Turbo-teaching zones

Pin back your ears and open your eyes – the turbo-teacher comes to the dais

A simple test question for the school of the future might well be, how close is its drama department to the centre of this school, both physically and figuratively? We should stop making assumptions about the nature and role of this subject. Drama should perhaps be re-branded as 'whole body learning' for this subject has the scope to be the carrier medium for most of the powerful new learning approaches we develop in the next few years. For learning at its most effective is often about physically doing and experiencing something.

Technology that fits with this notion of walk, talk, feel and learn is already with us. We find it with the now ubiquitous mobile phone, the MP3 player and even the Playstation. Such examples herald a new age of portable information and communication devices with instant relevance to the way that learning can take place. It really is time to think broad and deep and dramatically about how ICT will change the formality and the established blueprint for how learning takes place.

Some schools are starting to consider the development of one to very many teaching zones, with good projection and breakout areas for smaller group activity. For a start let's call this the turbo-teaching zone – please rename as appropriate until it feels right to you, but I quite like the ebullience of this description. The challenge then is to marry the tools of large group presentation with the space for drama and role play, such that from the large groups, small group breakout is possible and easily managed. In a turbo-teaching zone, a powerful presentation from a specialist will make a key area of learning come to life. This learning will then be reinforced and applied through practical activities which promote the use of a variety of media and encourage a range of contexts and styles for learning.

Suitable themes for turbo-teaching might include:

➡ The rudiments of geometry

➡ What is algebra really about?

➡ How to be web clever rather than web lazy – stop copying and start learning

➡ The history of the UK from 1066 to the present day.

The pole house rules

Learning a subject is in some ways like building a pole house. It requires the assembly of four or five key pillars of understanding on which the rest of the structure is built. We could start by asking each subject teacher what they would identify as the substructure to their specialism. This is an ideal activity to undertake with staff as part of a staff development day. It could be a day when we remove subject boundaries and look at the commonality of learning – a day when the values close to the heart of those who love their subject are shared, and where aspects of the subject that are considered most persuasive and sublime are shared between members of a profession, previously separated by the artificial packaging of knowledge. It could be a day when English teachers go home at ease with Heisenberg's uncertainty principle and science teachers are happy with the notion of hyperbole.

Once defined at school level in this way, we can look across the key substructural elements and look for commonality. We could treat the resultant list of essentials as the pillars on which all other learning will take place in the school. By doing so, a school is taking and reshaping its own platform of priorities for teaching and learning. These pillars of understanding can be taught, where possible, as common themes across each subject. The more frequently the learner encounters them, the more they will embed as the foundation of pupils' learning. A turbo-teaching event may be a useful way to return and re-emphasize them, for example, 'Tuesday lunchtime – the five pillars of physical geography'.

New grammars of teaching with these new tools will emerge through practice and experience at class level. A more subtle language of teaching and learning can be expected to develop among education professionals over time. This will dig beneath purely behavioural descriptions and express progression in more analytical terms. Diagnosis will never again be 'must try harder' but will more closely resemble the more anatomical explanations used by a general practitioner. A growing knowledge of the predispositions of learners and their response to different contexts and modes of learning will shape the capabilities of the education professional of the internet age.

Teachers will find their own point of access with the use of image, sound and moving video as part of their armoury for classroom exposition. The size of audience will not be a limiting factor if the teaching is incisive and dynamic. Good teaching will be less age specific. We know that, more or less, any subject can be explained to any audience. So good topics, explained well and making use of the best presentational formats, could be used up and down the school. Learning mentors could build on the key messages with differing techniques, appropriate to age, for embedding the learning. And where a key learning topic rides across subjects, and where a particular teacher has the skills and inclination to present it large, why shouldn't the whole-year group watch it?

In some ways, the grammar and the engagement of interactive cinema can now come to school. Students are familiar with sitting for two hours in a cinema when their style needs for intake, sound/light levels and comfortable seating are met effectively. Turbo-teaching is a way of taking this experience and making the most of it in school – a kind of school assembly with knobs on, a place where students are keen to go because they know the pace and entertainment value will be high. Events can be tailored in advance, optional lunchtime sessions offered and key life skills can be integrated into the programme up there on the big screen. Schools could have a 'coming soon' board. Five key life skills, including the uncut 'how to put up a shelf when you get your own place to live' or 'pancake day masterchef – see the famous show how they do it and then try yourself'. In addition, schools could consider the running of lunchtime premieres for work produced in-house using a variety of media (see Chapter 3).

Turbo-teaching could also include broadcasting to other schools via a sound file radio broadcast, live or recorded. Digital video of key moments may also be feasible, but a lot harder to manage and edit. Perhaps the ideal compromise is the soundtrack of an event linked to pictures and slides that are shown in the digital story-telling format.

A presentational goal for the turbo-teacher will be the 'pin your eyeballs back and watch, listen and feel the key points'. This will be a powerful illustrated overview – using the techniques of in-house sound and video editing, digital story-telling and animation to get the key points of a new module across to a large number rapidly. It would be followed up by deeper investigation in smaller class groups. Several schools are starting to digitize existing materials and important broadcast programmes with definitive subject context – these can then be used to form the bones of such a presentation.

Many teachers will jump at the chance to present a certain area of the curriculum in loud and proud mode. They will also be only too happy to leave other subjects which are not their area of specialism to other colleagues. Teachers will of course rise to the occasion, share ideas and learn from each other. This would also provide a useful staff development role in breaking down the isolation of pedagogy in the individual classroom. Teaching remains a collegiate activity, presenting a continuum of knowledge that does not suggest a quantized view of human experience, punctuated by bells and artificial boundaries.

Chapter 6

Staff & school development

▌What's in it for teachers?

Work within your own vision

Having a vision for using ICT to improve how we organize teaching and learning is the starting point for a journey of improvement. The big question is, 'how am I, as a teacher, going to translate aspiration into action?' Behind that question lies the fact that the classroom of the future is the one you will teach in tomorrow.

When we look across schools, we will generally find a similar range of ICT work taking place. There is still an emphasis in many schools on learning about software applications used in offices – word-processing, spreadsheets and databases. These applications have grown into large, complex tools and somehow schools have felt that students have to learn as much about them as possible in the time available.

The real opportunity to push learning forward with ICT will emerge as each school extends their use of new software tools and their knowledge of accelerated learning to do things differently, more creatively and more learner centred. The future will see schools build their own bespoke applications of new tools and environments to suit the teachers, students and their own particular school circumstances. This push on broadening the depth of experience for students by using ICT has already started in the UK, helping schools to leave behind our more utilitarian ideas of what ICT in schools is for.

The art of presentation

There are two main reasons why a range of presentation technologies have not become more prevalent in the classroom. They are the teacher's lack of time to build confidence, and the lack of appropriate training in their use. In many cases, this is compounded by the peripatetic work patterns of teachers, which means they can't set up their preferred system in any one classroom as they would wish. There is also a tendency, where educational technology is concerned, for schools to rush to the next new thing. This immediately demotes older technologies as out of date and therefore less effective. Too often, however, the reverse is true. Just because something becomes digitally possible doesn't mean that teachers have to graft it into the curriculum by nightfall.

There are many paths to using new software application tools effectively in whole-class teaching. Before we consider what tools might be deployed in front of the class in the shape of the computer, projector and interactive whiteboard, it is worth taking a step back to examine the role of a predecessor to the whiteboard – the overhead projector. One might be tempted to think that the OHP is obsolete technology in the wake of data projectors but the simple means to project transparencies and the ability to write on them is a powerful technology at a cost-effective price, with nothing to go wrong except a new bulb every few years. The OHP also exemplifies many of the issues and opportunities of technology integration in the classroom.

At less than £100, the OHP is a low cost resource ideal for sharing and showing graphical and textual information up high on the classroom wall in students' visual fields where the retention figure improves by 80 per cent for images shown above the mid-line.

To make effective use of resources, including overhead projectors and data projectors, teachers need to be confident in their use and they need to know they will find a machine clean and ready to work in all classrooms they are called to teach in. Only then is it worthwhile to invest time in producing resources.

Staff may need guidance on how to copy onto acetate transparencies via photocopier or laser printer. It's also useful to be shown how colour copies can be made via a bubblejet printer with reversed type, so the light literally shines through the letters on the page. It's also best if screens for OHPs and other types of projector are permanently fitted in a position so that all students can see. An ideal is a matt white painted board angled into the upper corner at the front right or left of the classroom, leaving the main whiteboard free for standard work.

Many teachers now use the second whiteboard as a 'bullet point catcher' – a place to record the big picture points as they emerge through the lesson. There is no reason why a classroom should not be fitted with three whiteboards. The first, a working area or scratchpad, the second, a source of stimulus (visual and auditory) and the third, a place to capture the conclusions.

Indeed, it is predictable that this trend will occur with the recognition that fewer students than teachers will have a strongly developed preference for learning by listening (unlike the teacher, who is often more than likely to be a 'radio person'). The words of wisdom that characterize a teacher's ideas of learning might remain in the mind of the teacher and some of her audience, but for most learners, ready and prepared for concrete learning experiences that don't come, such words float away into the ether, never to be heard again.

The OHP as staff training tool

Even if teachers have access to data projection from the computer and an interactive whiteboard for illustration – most of the key skills of how to show, engage and elucidate using images up in students' visual field, can be practised and developed with the use of the simple OHP. It is one of the simplest of projection technologies we have for making a difference for learners in the standard classroom and for engaging a variety of learning styles when linked to sound from a tape, CD or laptop.

In my first school, only the technology department had mastered the use of the overhead projector. They had a large roll of acetate on which they stored a complete term's worth of lessons. The teachers stood by the side of the machine and cranked the handle to bring up screen after screen of illustrated notes.

The students in the classes probably had too much of a good thing, for any technology can be overused, but the reality of the learning experience in most other classrooms was just the opposite. Elsewhere, and considering the prevalence of visual learning preferences in younger learners, the balance of modalities was heavily pitched towards speaking, listening and writing and away from seeing and doing.

New light through old windows

Digital resources from CD-ROM, the image scanner and the world wide web allow teachers to access and share resources. These can then be printed out on acetate, brought to the front of the classroom and turned into a big text and picture story. The acetate printed from these resources can serve as a bridgehead between the classroom and the world of infinite digital resources outside.

The overhead projector used with publishing or word-processing software allows teachers to build their own AV resources at low cost and link them to sound simply by playing tapes or a CD while a series of slides are shown.

Interestingly, this approach has much in common with the earliest public entertainment systems where slides and, later, jumpy black and white movies, were accompanied by a pianist providing the matching musical moods. Fast forward to today's classrooms and we can now see some of the most effective and moving 'digital stories' created by students involving little more than still frames accompanied by a soundtrack of voice and mood music.

Five ways to re-energize the OHP

➡ Set displays of words to music – drop key vocabulary onto the OHP as music plays at the end of a lesson.

➡ Subject trailers – 'coming soon' OHP revealed line by line like film titles.

➡ Cut up a key picture/scene and place it on the OHP bit by bit, asking students what, where, who it might be.

➡ Get students coming to the front to point out parts of the image/text on display.

➡ A 'teach one many learn' approach using word dominoes where students take a word to the front and add it to a word chain at a point where they can justify a connection in terms of meaning or a causal link.

➡ Provide staffroom access to a store of acetates for teacher use and a computer set up and reserved specifically to print worksheets/acetates from floppy disk.

Some of the early adopter members of our community tend to hunger for the latest of technologies. They will be the ones whose phones take pictures, play music, show television programmes and provide a spoken weather forecast every half hour. Owning an older technology in their presence can lead to scornful looks. We may feel slightly intimidated too by their technological superiority. But, experience and history tends to teach us a common lesson that it is best not to focus on one particular technology or tool in the classroom but to integrate and connect a variety. Coupled with that is the maxim that the simplest option is often the best. As for keeping up with the latest, it must be true that a device will continue to do what attracted us to it in the first place, even though something faster or different may now have emerged. If a choice of activity, which uses ICT, is effective in promoting good learning outcomes then we can feel fully confident in the choices we have made.

Integrating technology – some practical ideas

Many paths to the same destination

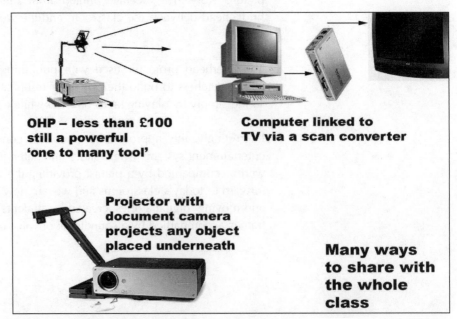

OHP – less than £100 still a powerful 'one to many tool'

Computer linked to TV via a scan converter

Projector with document camera projects any object placed underneath

Many ways to share with the whole class

Some teachers will want an OHP. Others will want a camera fixed over a platform so they can show objects and read books on the platter and have them appear on the screen. Any video camera with a yellow socket will do this when linked to a television with a compatible yellow phone socket (video) or a SCART port.

If you have access to a television with a video input – usually in the form of a SCART socket – you can display your computer signal using a scan converter. Don't worry about the language, it's just a small black box that converts the computer signal so it may be shown on the television screen or recorded onto videotape if you connect the box through a video recorder. This video option is particularly useful – some schools use it for putting pupil work such as PowerPoint presentations onto tapes for the students to take home.

At times, it's very helpful to provide access to easily managed sound – from cassette to CD to laptop to touch screen. There are at least four ways you can tie in music to a particular period of a lesson: by using concert review; to announce a break state – a short period of respite and relaxation; to announce the big picture; or for general cueing of a regular lesson part such as a summary or a brainstorm.

With technology there are always alternatives that can be used to suit the subject or lesson topic:

➡ For the English teacher – an electronic whiteboard may be the ideal tool for it allows flexibility in presentation and interaction with text, picture and internet source materials which they can annotate and connect during their exposition.

Electronic whiteboard

➡ For the technology teacher – an air mouse (a screen pointer that needs no wires or mouse pad) means they can move around class displaying key PowerPoint points on 'safety', or other themes, while not diverting their attention away from what students are doing.

Ultra Mouse (air mouse)

reproduced by permission of Gyration.

> ➡ For the maths teacher – a digitizer pad or a tablet PC will allow detailed, diagrammatic work that allows the teacher to face the class and retain eye contact.

Digitizer pad

Fuelling the vision within

ICT is likely to be a powerful agent for change as schools explore their own internal development priorities with teaching and learning styles and the role of accelerated learning techniques. Now is the time for a hand on the tiller at school level to turn what we now know about ICT and learning into practical action. How should we make the most of our ICT hardware and software tools? Perhaps in the early days the focus had drifted too much towards the personal and hands on use of technology, and away from the whole-group mediation and story-telling from the front of the classroom. Now there is also the danger that the pendulum will swing too far the other way and with projection and interactive whiteboards we will feed the 'greedy cortex' of the visual field and miss the chance to build the muscles of listening by dimming the lights and tuning into a live reading or a recorded story.

Each school's vision, which will embody their values, is uniquely important because that is the place and context in which students and teachers have to live and work. Part of the challenge for schools is to hold their nerve and develop their own unique approach. The best advice is to look at what others are doing but also to reflect and make up your own minds about what is best for you.

Ways forward for schools, staff and student learning curves

A key responsibility for schools and senior management, in particular, is building a vision for their school in the future and following it up with successful development planning. The challenge is to make the most of the potential catalytic force where knowledge about learning, infused with new tools for communication, might help us to avoid falling into the trap of following a single technology, or approach, to the exclusion of all others.

The future development path of schools looks likely to be relentlessly portable and connected, bringing opportunities to link schools to resources in the world outside. There is a home to school to work explosion on its way. Continuity will become the next big feature to promote in education – continuity of learning from classroom to home, and continuity of progression in learning from school to the workplace. The former will benefit from how we learn and the latter will benefit by what we learn, for the skills necessary to make intelligent and effective use of ICT are also the skills most sought after in young people by employers.

As we saw in Chapter 5, we have the opportunity to learn from the past as well as the future. Technology does not always provide us with radically different possibilities. It is sometimes a replay of something we had before with some different features. When personal computers suddenly had chips that could go fast enough to play full screen motion video, we heralded this to be a breakthrough. Then came the recognition that we had just reinvented television. Similarly, the development of the laptop computer into a tablet PC that we could write on, was really a reincarnation of the slate with knobs on. This is not a cynical observation because a digital slate is truly a wonderful thing in being able to link with the rest of the digital world of information. It's just that we don't need to throw away everything we know each time new technology comes along – for it is likely to be something old and familiar, dressed in smart new clothes.

Sometime during the history of the development of ICT in UK schools, the computer room was invented. It was necessary to do this because we had only 30 computers but a thousand students and rationing was the order of the day. Although some students will seek to study ICT to a specialist level, the main thrust of ICT in schools is to use ICT as a tool for learning in all subjects of the curriculum, and to develop an essential capability for a majority of studies, and vocations beyond school. In many schools, to make use of ICT requires the booking of an ICT room and moving the class there at the requisite time. However, think of the slightly nonsensical situation that would exist if pens were rationed like computers, and students had to go to a 'pen room' in order to record their ideas.

The pen was a very early form of information technology. Luckily it is ubiquitous and can be slipped from the pocket whenever needed. Computers are the modern equivalent of the pen – only much more flexible and powerful. But it is also obvious that one day soon every pupil will have their personal wireless computer just like they now all have a pen – or a mobile phone. So, beyond the computer room there is a more convenient future where computers will be available at the place of learning wherever that may be.

In the future, computers will not need to stay in one place. Many schools now use mobile sets of wireless laptop computers in flexible ways that are well integrated with other learning activities. Across the world, notably in New Zealand, Australia and the USA, the dominant use of ICT as a tool rather than a subject is moving planning away from the notion of ICT rooms. With the de-centralization of ICT in schools comes new opportunities of working with a variety of learning style needs and the chance to engage students at new depths of learning, exploration and creativity. Once we match the needs, dynamics and opportunities for learning styles and accelerated learning to ICT tools, the next stage is to distil and refine local provision. Schools themselves are best placed to decide how best to deploy technology to assist, accelerate and to make the learning process more insightful and delightful.

▌Whole-school planning and integration of new tools for learning

Doing ICT for themselves

Sweyne Park School in Essex, UK is passionate about using ICT to share work and resources in classrooms. For the last three years it has brought work to the front of the classroom by connecting classroom computers to large television monitors.

After a successful pilot scheme, some departments have now received data projectors in their classrooms to take this work further. Regular demonstration sessions where staff show others what they are doing have ensured that good ideas spread quickly.

Once a year they run a staff training session for each other. The day is slightly unusual because it's run by staff for staff. One year, in one room, the head of humanities ran a course on web page making, while in another, the head of ICT was running a seminar on digital video editing.

In yet another session, staff were shown how to take pictures, annotate them and store them on the school server for students to access. The day had begun with five members of staff from different departments giving a short presentation on how they were using ICT and the school network to publish work and share ideas.

Each member of staff attended three of the activities and their finished work was published on the school intranet and taken back to school to provide exemplar material for further work.

For schools integrating ICT to help accelerate learning, the challenge is not to let a thousand uses bloom but to develop the learning environment so that different learning styles are catered for and students can demonstrate their understanding using tools suited to a range of particular capabilities. Some teachers will use staff room printouts and OHP slides in class – some will use the internet live, projected onto an interactive whiteboard. Ultimately, the development and application of new tools in the classroom will be a local event and the confidence which allows teachers to make the most of the opportunities requires ongoing personal and professional development.

Art of the state

At times, it might seem as though many other schools are racing ahead with innovative uses of ICT because it is always the high profile and leading edge examples that get the publicity. Other schools might have wall-to-wall interactive whiteboards and ICT learning centres while your school may still be trying to get aspects of basic provision right. The advice here is to hold your nerve, for each individual school's chosen path doesn't have to be state of the art – for this really means little in an education context. What we really want is to be art of the state. That is, to use a variety of teaching approaches and ICT props to manage the state of optimum learning for students with a variety of learning styles and needs.

Large screen projection, independent access and local stores of mediated knowledge in shared folders will undoubtedly be important in developing this provision. Each iteration towards the local sharing and celebrating of knowledge will be unique at school level.

Taking it further

A simple audit of the contribution that ICT makes to different learning style needs in the classroom is a useful way to focus on present provision in individual schools.

Matching the technology to the learning style

You can use the following questions to help you ascertain the ways in which different learning styles are facilitated by the deployment of a range of learning technologies and activities. All questions relate to school networks/standalone machines and portables as appropriate. Score one point for every answer of three or more.

1. How many pieces of software are there for writing/word-processing?
2. How many pieces of software are there for working with images?
3. How many pieces of software are there for the recording and editing of sound?
4. How many ways are there of editing still and moving images?
5. How many places are there where you can scan in a piece of artwork/drawing?
6. How many ways are there of publishing work for others to see within the school community, and beyond for parents and others?
7. How many places can students go to proof listen to some digital text?

What types of answers do you get? If you returned a score of less than five points, your provision may indeed be skewed towards those that are print clever – that is students already benefiting from text on the page as they are enjoying further opportunities on screen.

Suggested follow-up activity for teachers

In small groups (cross-curricular if possible), spend 20 minutes discussing opportunities to broaden the access to learning activities beyond text based approaches – review the guidance on zoning in Chapter 6 and matching ICT to VAK in Chapter 2 to help you.

List your own short- and long-term objectives

Use a table with headings like this to list short- and long-term objectives for supporting various learning styles with ICT tools.

Current provision	Short-term objectives	Long-term objectives

▌Contentions

The following contentions should be read out and discussed in small groups.

Contention 1

The fulcrums for learning are the mouth, ears, hands and eyes. Yet up till now investment in ICT has given us silence, a strange spatially challenging interface using a mouse and some text. Around school networks – which have cost up to £100,000 to install – runs text, served mainly in silence, to many learners.

We know that many pupils learn best through an interplay of image, sound, activity and movement. Pupils interact with up to five hours of visual media each day and are experts at decoding multimedia information rapidly. Furthermore, the decoding of text is strongly centred in left brain processing as reading is a highly analytical activity. Certain learners who are 'good with text' have the keys to most learning opportunities with the old and the new tools. But what price is paid and what unfairness is present for those who prefer to learn in a more diverse and creative way?

Is it now time to work beyond the sensory mismatch between learning strengths and needs of students and the tools and technologies we deploy to work with them?

Contention 2

I think like a lot of teachers, I used to be a "control freak". I liked to stand at the front and make sure I'd explained very carefully to all the students exactly what they needed to know by the end of the lesson then they commenced to write it down. I can see that I preferred a didactic approach in my lessons. ICT has certainly encouraged me to produce learning activities where the students have to go and find out things rather than listen to what I am going to tell you sort of lesson. I think I am now getting a balance between the two sorts of lesson.

Chemistry teacher, Arkwright Secondary School – *Learning at Home and School Report*, BECTA (2002)

Contention 3

From a learner's point of view, software often matures past the point of best fit. As a piece of software is developed it gets better, and then it gets ruined by extra developments and complexity. The law of less is more ware means that education development of software tools continues through new versions to a point where it goes past its high tide of cognitive access for learners. When was the last time you found an extra feature you really needed in your standard word–processing program? What percentage of the features in your word processor do you use, or will you ever use?

Sometimes with software there can be too much of a good thing

Less is more ware

It is worth giving specific examples here. Perhaps the most ubiquitous of software, Microsoft Word now has over 200 features, of which most users will comfortably get by using only a small percentage. The result is an unnecessarily bloated and confusing program. Macromedia Flash is a program that lets you build animations. Version four was probably the best developed in terms of ease of use and access for learners under nine years old. But the developers couldn't give in to their urges to 'improve' it. Now we have versions that number eight and beyond, and the level of conceptual access is now unforgivingly high. So much so that what was looking like a slick creative tool for young learners has now ruled itself out of bounds. PaintShop Pro, an easy to use photo editing program, has gone the same way. Simple perfection was reached at version five when Animation Shop was included to shepherd young learners through the simple construction of animated GIFs. But now it has elevated itself for use only by a 'cleverer' group of people. What price consumer power against commercial pressure to upgrade to the latest version or be left behind and unsupported?

Computer applications will play a transformational role in the learning process only if driven by clear educational objectives rather than steered by the 'wisdom' of the developers. Sometimes we work this out for ourselves. There has been considerable publicity around digital video and governments and companies have both supported its use in schools – only to see schools work out for themselves that simple step by step animation was simpler, could happen in a short lesson time frame and had more powerful learning outcomes.

Now gather your own reflective quotes on changed practice and aspirations for the use of ICT as a learning tool. Quotes should begin with strong sensory verbs: I feel…, I think that…, I can see that…, We believe that… . Write your quotes on four separate Post-it notes and put them on the aspiration wall – a designated area where the caretaker won't mind. Now in groups, take ten minutes to read the aspiration wall.

Statistical scaffolding for ICT development

Whenever possible, search out the statistics and use them to inform future development and investment of ICT. Several schools and colleges allow students to book computer access in half hour slots in their resource centres. Some use cloth covers that are folded down over the screen saying, 'Book me if you wish to use me.' Through the booking system, managers can keep detailed statistics on the use of machines. If the machines have a particular purpose, for example, internet access or a talking word processor, then the data collected will indicate the most frequent types of use. Through such an audit can the expansion of types of ICT activity, through further investment, be justified.

Feedback informs future practice

Training ideas and opportunities

Consider an internally organized training day with the following outline:

Morning: Where we are and where we could go with ICT?

➡ What does our audit of ICT use tell us about the range of uses of ICT and the impact upon learning in subjects? Presentation by senior staff.

➡ What do we know about learning preferences? Presentation by working group.

➡ In developing the school's ICT work, what are the key things we should aim to achieve? Discussion in mixed groups.

➡ What single ICT development would each department identify as likely to make a difference to the quality of learning in their subject? Discussion in subject groupings.

Afternoon: Sharing our current ICT achievements – an ideas fair

Each department hosts a practical slot on how they use ICT resources in their teaching, with emphasis on why these uses are valuable to learning in this subject, followed by the opportunity for discussion. After one hour, staff change over so that everyone gets to see some ideas in action and to share ideas about organization and so on. Small development grants could be made available to departments if possible to enable their plans to be followed up.

Some schools build on this approach and make it into a whole day event. One half of the staff stay in their departments and prepare for visits from the other half of the school staff, showing them how they use ICT in their subject. In the afternoon the situation reverses and the visitors then play host in their own departments. Within a day, all teachers are thus able to see and learn from their colleagues – often more valuable than hearing even the most illustrious visiting speaker.

Vision framer – a staff development activity

The following is a suggested staff development activity.

In groups of four, read through each of the following scenarios. Place each scenario on a sliding scale (see scoring system below) for desirability and feasibility. Follow up this activity with a discussion on how it might be possible to make some of these ideas happen in school.

Scoring

Desirability

1 = Would be really useful to learning
5 = Little value for learners – a gimmick

Feasibility

1 = Pipe dream
5 = Could do it easily

Scenarios

1. Staff keep an eye on the screen in the corner of the staffroom as the daily news is broadcast over the school network by a team of volunteers and GCSE media students. The weather is a particularly hotly debated spot as students interpret a downloaded satellite weather image and present it with labels on a blue screen studio wall. Archived news files mean that it's possible to relive previous famous newscasts that have now passed into school folklore.

2. John has met his short-term subject based targets for the third time. A text message is sent automatically by the school intranet system to his mother's and father's mobile phones. All letters to parents are by email (as well as hard copy) with automatic acknowledgements returned when they have been read.

3. As you walk into school in the morning you meet Saima who is the internet monitor this week. She has just printed out the visible satellite picture of Europe taken from space at 6.00am that morning and is pinning it to the notice board in the foyer under the sign saying, 'This morning up in space a picture was taken.' Next she will log all the answers written on the internet search board and type them into a

database so that they may be searched again in the future. Images from a field trip to the Isle of Arran are added to the intranet and a separate image database so in the future they may be searched using keywords when, for example, someone needs a picture of a 'U' shaped valley.

WEBSITE

4. Parents log on to the QCA site (www.ncaction.co.uk) to see the type of work that students need to do to get a level 6 at KS3 in English. Having shown this to their child, the student now has a vocabulary of expectation as to what a good piece of work looks like at that level. The parents too know what to expect and are able to offer a level of home support.

5. Parents gather around a laptop and speaker set up in the foyer as part of a school radio display. Each minute the latest school news is broadcast in a different language so that mothers and fathers present hear a little of the latest news in the life of the school in their mother tongue.

Activity – identifying ICT skills as a teacher

As ICT develops in schools, teachers find out things about using ICT that work well for them. Collectively, a whole staff will have a large repertoire of ideas that would be well worth sharing with colleagues. The following activity encourages sharing.

Allocate a pinboard where staff can advertise an ICT skill, technique or tip that they find useful in the classroom either directly (for example, something to do with how to use a data projector) or indirectly (a tip about producing a worksheet before the lesson). Staff advertise the details of the skill and the stage someone should be at before they could find it easy to adopt, for example, should possess good word-processing skills.

At this point, half the group of the teachers should select a feature that they would like to know about and the author of the tip then spends up to 20 minutes showing their colleagues how to do it and discussing the impact it has had. Now rotate the exercise and have those who were shown a feature then demonstrate something that they know that works for them.

The exercise can end with a small group brainstorm on how staff can continue to share the learning recipe as ICT continues to develop in the school.

Broadening the repertoire

Each teacher can broaden their repertoire of ICT use by investigating, in a non-threatening environment, new possibilities for using the tools of our time. The next activity encourages teaching staff to do just that.

Consider some key resources currently used for instruction. Rate all the tools that staff use and find most helpful in their teaching, in order of importance. Conduct a spot survey with each member of staff. Ask them to rate the following on a scale of 1 to 5 (5 being essential, 1 would make a nice optional extra, 0 being never heard of it). Examples would include: laptop computer, scanner, digital camera, microphone projector, OHP, interactive whiteboard and so on.

Publish the results up on a data projector in Excel with a bar chart to show the highest and lowest scoring tools, or make an acetate for the OHP. A second ranking exercise should then be conducted for generic software – word processor, sound editing, video editing and so on.

Finally, sort the feedback by highest score to find the staff favourites. Use these results and pointers which follow from the discussion as a consideration in medium-term planning.

Activity – VAK: Matching activities to particular learning preferences

Pass around a hat containing a number of folded up pieces of paper with a teaching objective written on each one. Then pass around another hat with separate learning modalities identified on different pieces of paper. Teachers in groups of three or four then take a piece of paper from each hat. Their task is to devise an activity which they could use to emphasize the particular learning modality in the way that students learned it. For example:

Teaching objective	Learning modality
Causes for the Second World War	Auditory
Chronology	Tactile
Molecule in liquid solid gas states	Visual

Developing these concepts – questions to consider

➡ How could we extend these ideas when planning a scheme of work?

➡ What features would you find in a lesson designed to employ a range of styles of learning?

➡ What part can ICT play in supporting these learning opportunities?

At the close of the event some upbeat music could be played and a Word document containing the key points and images from the day scrolled on screen using a wheel mouse.

Thinking and training tools for ICT and learning

The following ideas should be thought of as a set of free-form thinking tools to be used as and when you see fit. They could be used in a supportive investigative environment to acknowledge fears, encourage sharing (an end to individual cleverness) and allow staff to find their own point of access.

At times, staff will be content to hover in helicopter overview, seeing the terrain but not engaging totally with any particular part. At other times, they will be celebrating the time saving amplifier of the DIOUIM effect (do it once use it many). Finally, as the school grows collectively smarter, individual teachers will document their capability in new tool making by using screenshots/screen recordings or live seminars to show how they did it – for this is a key algorithm of potential group improvement, and a way of sharing the learning recipe.

Helicopter and hands on approaches

There are no natural limits to what a learner can achieve when conditions, resources and the environment are right. We know that ICT, used in the right way, can be a catalyst in promoting the capacity to learn. This will only happen however if both teachers and students feel confident to take risks and follow their instinctive learning patterns and approaches with these new tools.

But we will only make the most of the opportunity if the learner and teacher are empowered rather than undermined and over stressed. A tip for easing the tension of a hesitant user is to point out the confidence inducing 'undo' command.

Positioning yourself for most effective learning opportunities with ICT

Choose your position – helicopter or hands on?

If you understand to your satisfaction the complete workings and potential of the software, system or tool then you might consider the level of your interaction to be ground level hands on. A close up gardening 'hands in the soil' type of approach where you can see and feel and understand how this tool or technique might grow and be propagated.

At other times, the complexity of sequence, or number of steps which a particular technology or approach may require, can steeple upwards and out of your immediate understanding or technical grasp. That uncomfortable feeling of losing a close conceptual grip on the area being examined might just begin to well up. This is likely to be the case if there is a substantial mismatch between your learning need and the manner of instruction. For instance, you might have a tactile or kinesthetic learning preference so if someone else is holding the mouse and talking you through, it won't really be much help. Be aware while you are teaching and being taught what approaches work best for you.

At such moments, feel free to hitch a ride in your personal helicopter. Get above the technology and its various iterations and enjoy the comfort and the wider viewpoint of an elevated perspective.

Talk around the machine – a key tool in understanding

1. *Get students to work together on a machine so that they can talk and pole-bridge each other by describing exactly what they are doing as they use the computer. Use an egg timer (real or digital) to announce handover points where keyboard and mouse control switches between learners.*

2. *Use cardboard traffic lights on top of monitors to get feedback on how learners are progressing, for example, green when students are in the flow – amber for slightly challenged – red for stuck.*

3. *Tell stories as a way to share the learning recipe of how best to use the computer – 'I'm now going down into the hard disk, I may be some time.'*

Telling stories as a learning tool
Story-telling provides a fast track to cognitive access at times and can be used as a subtle and non-threatening coaching device. Stories carry meaning, reduce threat and make concepts accessible.

The parable of the hard drive – where am I in relation to my resources?
Let us consider for a moment the story of the 'A' drive. When the first computer was invented, it needed a storage device. So a large external magnetic disk drive was added and the 'A' drive was born. Moving on through the mists of digital time, let us consider perhaps a female boffin who had a dream in the night of expanded capacity and, in the morning, added a second floppy drive to the computer giving us the 'B' drive. Much later, another breakthrough saw the arrival of the hard drive and the letter 'C' got used.

Many years pass and then Phillips invented the compact disc and the 'D' drive was born – unless perchance you had two hard drives in which case the 'E' drive was born. Now, just to complicate matters, let us plug into a network, which adds virtual drives where programs and students' work could be stored. We are now into the realms of the completely exotic having drive names such as 'L', 'M', 'N' and 'P'.

Finally, consider the internet to be a network of networks in which every computer connected has its own postal address, known as an internet protocol number or IP address. If you want to call another user up over the internet for a videoconference say, you would use this in the same way that you would a phone number.

One of the biggest challenges for new users of computers is making sure documents are filed in the right place. New users are identified by their habit of proclaiming that the computer has 'lost their file'. More experienced users know that this is a clear sign that they need a little help with file handling. Time spent on this with staff and students is worthwhile – a chance for misconceptions to surface and be considered and everyone to get comfortable. But more importantly, no one need think they have lost valuable work if conceptually they understand where they are depositing their files when using the less than intuitive filing system that sits on every computer.

Digital concrete

Much of the potential of ICT as a learning tool may be lost if teachers and students don't have a chance to build their own models and metaphors as to how new tools and the medium of ICT works. For many, the mysteries of the technology may be unwrapped by approaches which gives the virtual world some physical reference in the 'real world'. For others, the first breakthrough might come when they start to own the language that is used to describe these new tools.

Concrete examples defuse threat and make understanding simpler in the world of virtual tools of desktops, recycling bins and operating systems – and work stored on hard drives with strange postal addresses, such as 'p:/public/teacher/worksheets'.

Where possible, give printers and hard drives a name that carries some association for users. This is easier on the Apple Mac but possible on all types of computer and it makes a real difference as memory works in part through association and the name of an island, for example, is easier to remember than the letter 'P'.

We can also articulate the internet as a system of connected computers down which various file types travel. One way to teach this in a tangible way is to use string to show the connection between various points of communication. Clothes pegs can be labelled as JPEG files (images) and MP3 files and so on and moved along the string to simulate multimedia web pages being called up from the internet to the computer desktop. Such simplicity of interpretation may seem trivial, but it is an important premise to show that nothing is really complicated. Technology only seems complicated because sometimes we fail to make the effort needed to explain it simply.

Let's get physical

The challenge is to give students and staff secure metaphors of how these new tools work. A common assumption is that all staff/students know how a network works and where work is stored – many will not and this will prevent their making the most adventurous use. Problems increase for some with the dawn of wireless networking – where is my work and where are resources stored – how can I get back to it?

The more virtual the learning experience becomes, the greater effort we must make to find a real life concrete correlation or comparison. Seeing and making connections are the first steps towards understanding and getting braver and more adventurous in the use of these new tools. Time spent providing many paths to understanding how ICT tools work and may be utilized is time well spent. For learners will be disenfranchised if they are unable to build their own models and ideas on how they might use and learn with the learning prosthetic tools of our time.

Research bursaries

Many schools now provide teachers with resources and time so that they can explore a research task. Usually, the teachers select an investigation into a process which might improve the quality of the learning experience. Areas of exploration are likely to be diverse – perhaps the use of school radio as a revision and review tool or the use of video along with active viewing sheets to guide note taking.

Assessment joins the ICT revolution

In the future, assessment will be unobtrusive, sophisticated and will be better at measuring what students learn, rather than how well they respond to the context of the test. Learning in the future will not need to be geared to the test. Students will not need to spend half their final year in a school rehearsing exam techniques.

Mike Bostock, ICT education consultant

Assessment, not surprisingly, tends to drive what schools teach. At primary school level, the three tests used to measure pupils' levels in just three subjects (English, mathematics and science) have tended to elevate the importance of those three subjects over everything else a primary school might do. The breadth of achievement of young learners that was once a characteristic of the best practice at this level has been rendered down to just three numbers. Interesting, too, how a knowledge-based subject, science, found its way onto the list. Surely if we are choosing core skills as the foundation for learning we would choose literacy, numeracy and ICT.

In the secondary school, the gatekeeper to the careers and rewards that lie beyond school is the GCSE examination. A few hours of solitary writing in a silent room remains the method of judging 16 previous years of rich multi-modal learning.

A new approach to assessment in the British education system is probably now overdue. Developments in online testing are making more sophisticated use of ICT for calculating a broader profile of what pupils can do rather than the primitive multiple-choice marking of the past. The future is in assessment systems which integrate seamlessly with the learning activity and provide continual formative feedback and adaptive learning programmes.

Such a system that integrates the measurement, or 'metrics', of learning with content delivery, providing feedback to teacher and learner, and creating a statistical profile of progress throughout the course, would be an effective new tool for learning. Given the administrative overload that many teachers are experiencing, it is probably time to intelligently automate assessment. There are software programs that can now mark essays with greater consistency than human markers. It is also time to muffle the big bang of summative assessment in favour of gathering progression information and providing feedback to the learner throughout the course.

Summative assessment does little to help the individual student improve. As Vygotsky might say, the process does nothing to contribute to work in that fertile area – the student's zone of proximal development where a child's emergent capability resides. Inexorably, if we follow the research beacons, the focus will fall on the 'hand to tiller opportunities' provided by formative assessment.

Formative evaluation is, in a sense, feedback on the hoof to help learners get better while they learn. There is much potential for the process to be assisted by the record keeping strengths and the perfect digital accuracy that database driven ICT resources could provide. Just imagine during a task that students see their name automatically appear on an interactive whiteboard for asking a good question.

Feedback to learner while learning is still going on

Soon we will stop using pen and paper to test ability and potential and start using database tools to gather performance information in a range of media. For these new skills can no longer be confined to this format. The subtlety of a musical composition, or the invention of an animation on an historical event, need to be appreciated in the media format of their construction and responded to in a vocabulary we don't at present possess.

We have the greatest opportunity to make a positive difference for individual students through the development of formative assessment. Research by Professor Black among others has shown that innovations which include strengthening the practice of formative assessment produce significant and often substantial learning gains.

Current assessment practice measures progress in relation to national curriculum subject outcomes. Work to date shows that it is also possible to place measures on attributes that have no intrinsic units, for example, 'students' views on their learning'. Such work can provide a personalized learning profile for each pupil, tracking progress in each area against learning targets. At any stage, students can review their learning progress profile and their new targets. ICT can automate much of the collection, diagnosis and presentation of information. Individual learning targets can be automatically generated, with teacher mediation if needed. The greatest irony perhaps is that as a novice buyer and seller on the Ebay auction site I already have a substantial formative assessment profile.

Ebay user's feedback form

Member Profile: aardvarkwisdom (29 ☆)

Feedback Score:	**29**
Positive Feedback:	**100%**
Members who left a positive:	29
Members who left a negative:	0
All positive feedback received:	30

Learn about what these numbers mean.

Recent Ratings:

		Past Month	Past 6 Months	Past 12 Months
⊕	positive	1	3	8
⊙	neutral	0	0	0
⊖	negative	0	0	0

Bid Retractions (Past 6 months): 0

All Feedback Received	**From Buyers**	**From Sellers**	**Left for Others**

30 feedback received by aardvarkwisdom (0 mutually withdrawn)

Comment	From
⊕ Would do business with again. Quick payer.	Seller philmartindale1 (2)
⊕ Very prompt payment.Highly recommended E-bayer.A+++++	Seller shado1963 (122 ☆)
⊕ Paid in cash - excellent & smooth transaction - recommend to anyone! Thankyou!!!	Seller man-from-mitsi (1)
⊕ Good ebayer! Hoping to service you again!!!A+++++++	Seller power_god (132 ☆) no longer a registered user
⊕ Excellent transaction, easy to deal with and a pleasure to meet ! A+++++++++++	Seller giles-chapman (19 ☆)

An Ebay user has more formative feedback available as soon as the first item is bought or sold and feedback is received than most children can access after 14 years of education.

Companies already use database driven approaches to track our shopping patterns and behaviours in such applications as loyalty cards. Perhaps it is inevitable that we will adopt the same techniques for learning, because learning must be as important as shopping. The opportunity to diagnose patterns, reinforce connections and suggest changes to the process is already on the high street; we ought to claim it for the classroom too!

For example, as a student walks through the school gates, a text message arrives on her phone, 'You seem to learn best when you begin a module with a discussion – there are three optional discussions scheduled in school today which you might be interested in.'

Conclusion

There is a genuine hunger to know more about the brain, how learning works and how best to use the technological tools of our time. Schools want to share and validate this potential. Yet we have also learned from experience that developments with technology should be underpinned by the recognition that the ultimate learning resource is human. It is another learner, or the teacher arriving at the corner of your desk at the moment that your cognitive penny is refusing to drop. Our Cro-Magnon processors may have changed little in the last 40,000 years, but we can use modern day know-how to provide a context where they may adapt and thrive.

Pigments, axes and spears have all had an upgrade in the world we now know but we are still toolmakers. We can now tap into a bigger brain and observe large moving interactive images flitting across the cave wall of the modern classroom. Our sticks in the sand were swapped with pens, and for a long time the values of education were firmly tied up in the craft skills of their use. To be able to listen, read and write stills marches on the higher ground of what is valued in education. But ICT changes the rules. It tells us that to force pupils to use exclusively the older technologies of pens, books and voice is to place a class filter on the richness of individuality, and to lead many to apparently underachieve. In the world beyond school, the skills and attributes that are needed in the jobs of tomorrow do not always strongly connect with what schools place greatest value upon today, and in some notable key areas cannot be found anywhere in our national curriculum. But that's another story.

In our search for digital longitude we have already travelled far. In education, the true revolution has begun, not so much from the march of technology into classrooms but from the growing confidence of teachers to challenge some of the assumptions about ICT, and for schools to actively explore the relationship between new tools and effective learning.

We have lived, so far, in heady days of digital promise, still seeking fulfilment within our learning institutions. Perhaps we have been steered for a little too long by technology instead of being guided by the surer compass of developments in our understanding of how people learn. Now our digital longitude awaits to be reinvented by individual schools to meet their needs and triangulated between environment, learning styles and new tools.

References

Chapter 1

Sobel, Dava (1995), *Longitude*, Fourth Estate (reprinted by permission of HarperCollins Ltd)

Warlick, David (2004), speaking at SETT's Learning and literacy in the twenty-first century – aka redefining literacy for a new century conference, Glasgow, Scotland, September

Wells, Gordon (1981), *The Meaning Makers: Children learning language and using language to learn*, Heinemann

Chapter 2

Abbott, John and Ryan, Terry (2000), *The Unfinished Revolution: Learning, human behaviour, community and political paradox*, Network Educational Press

Bruner, J. (1966), *Towards a Theory of Instruction*, Harvard University Press

Clarke, Arthur C. (1999), *Profiles of the Future*, Orion Paperbacks (reprinted by permission of David Higham Associates Ltd)

Comenius, J.A. (1649), *Didactica Magna*

Dunn, Rita (2000), *Learning styles: Theory, research, and practice*, National Forum of Applied Educational Research Journal, 13, (1), 3-22.

Gardner, Howard (1983), *Frames of Mind: The theory of multiple intelligences*, New York: Basic Books

Harrison, Chris (2004), speaking about formative assessment at ALT's Learning and Teaching Conference, Moray, Scotland, May

Postman, N. (1992), *Technopoly: The surrender of culture to technology*, Knopf

Race, Phil (1996), *Never Mind the Teaching – Feel the Learning*, Paper 80, Staff and Educational Development Association

Rose, Colin (1992), *Accelerated Learning*, Accelerated Learning Systems

Chapter 3

Aldrich, F. and Sheppard, L. (2000), *'Graphicacy: the fourth "R"?'* Primary Science Review, 64, (ASE 2000) pages 8–11

Björk (2002), BBC Radio 3 interview, May

Edwards, Betty (1989), *Drawing on the Right Side of the Brain – an exercise in reconnection and new ways of looking*, HarperCollins (reprinted by permission of HarperCollins Ltd)

Illich, Ivan (1970), *Deschooling Society*, Marion Boyars

Penrose, Sir Roger, quoted in Highfield, Roger (2003), 'Doodling "can draw on powers of thought"', *The Daily Telegraph*, 3 October

Prashnig, B. (2004), *The Power of Diversity*, Network Educational Press

Rankin, Oona (2003), *The Daily Telegraph*, 28 October, page 16

Chapter 4

Berners-Lee, Tim, © 7 May 1998, A one-page personal history of the web, Tim Berners-Lee, http://www.w3.org/People/BernersLee/ShortHistory.html, World Wide Web Consortium, (Massachusetts Institute of Technology, European Research Consortium for Informatics and Mathematics, Keio University)

Caxton, William (1475), *Recuyell of the Histories of Troye*

DfES (2003), *Fulfilling the Potential*, www.dfes.gov.uk/ictinschools/publications

McLuhan, Marshall (1962), *The Gutenberg Galaxy*, University of Toronto Press

Naughton, John (2004), A little e-learning is a dangerous thing, *The Observer*, 24 March © Guardian Newspaper Limited 2004

Chapter 5

Koch, John (2005), pole house designer, jkoch@labyrinth.net.au

Morris, Henry (1930s), speech at the opening of Impington Village College, Cambridgeshire (reproduced from the Encyclopedia of Informal Education, www.infed.org)

November, Alan (2004), East of England Broadband Conference, UK

Chapter 6

BECTA (2002), *Learning at Home and School Report*

Comber, C., et al. (2002), ImpaCT2: *Learning at Home and School: case studies*. Coventry: Becta/London: DfES http://www.becta.org.uk/research/impact2

Index

Other publications from Network Educational Press

ACCELERATED LEARNING SERIES

Accelerated Learning: A User's Guide by Alistair Smith, Mark Lovatt & Derek Wise
Accelerated Learning in the Classroom by Alistair Smith
Accelerated Learning in Practice by Alistair Smith
The ALPS Approach: Accelerated Learning in Primary Schools by Alistair Smith & Nicola Call
The ALPS Approach Resource Book by Alistair Smith & Nicola Call
ALPS StoryMaker by Stephen Bowkett
MapWise by Oliver Caviglioli & Ian Harris
Creating an Accelerated Learning School by Mark Lovatt & Derek Wise
Thinking for Learning by Mel Rockett & Simon Percival
Reaching out to all learners by Cheshire LEA
Move It: Physical movement and learning by Alistair Smith
Coaching Solutions by Will Thomas & Alistair Smith

ABLE AND TALENTED CHILDREN COLLECTION

Effective Provision for Able and Talented Children by Barry Teare
Effective Resources for Able and Talented Children by Barry Teare
More Effective Resources for Able and Talented Children by Barry Teare
Challenging Resources for Able and Talented Children by Barry Teare
Enrichment Activities for Able and Talented Children by Barry Teare
Parents' and Carers' Guide for Able and Talented Children by Barry Teare

LEARNING TO LEARN

Let's Learn How to Learn: Workshops for Key Stage 2 by UFA National Team
Brain Friendly Revision by UFA National Team
Creating a Learning to Learn School by Toby Greany & Jill Rodd
Teaching Pupils How to Learn by Bill Lucas, Toby Greany, Jill Rodd & Ray Wicks

PRIMARY RESOURCES

Promoting Children's Well-Being in the Primary Years: The Right from the Start Handbook
    edited by Andrew Burrell and Jeni Riley
But Why? Developing philosophical thinking in the classroom by Sara Stanley with Steve Bowkett
Foundations of Literacy by Sue Palmer & Ros Bayley
Help Your Child To Succeed by Bill Lucas & Alistair Smith
Help Your Child To Succeed – Toolkit by Bill Lucas & Alistair Smith
That's English! by Tim Harding
That's Maths! by Tim Harding
That's Science! by Tim Harding
The Thinking Child by Nicola Call with Sally Featherstone
The Thinking Child Resource Book by Nicola Call with Sally Featherstone
Numeracy Activities Key Stage 2 by Afzal Ahmed & Honor Williams
Numeracy Activities Key Stage 3 by Afzal Ahmed, Honor Williams & George Wickham

EXCITING ICT

Exciting ICT in Maths by Alison Clark-Jeavons
Exciting ICT in English by Tony Archdeacon
Exciting ICT in History by Ben Walsh

CREATIVE THINKING

Think it–Map it! by Ian Harris & Oliver Caviglioli
Thinking Skills & Eye Q by Oliver Caviglioli, Ian Harris & Bill Tindall
Reaching out to all thinkers by Ian Harris & Oliver Caviglioli
With Drama in Mind by Patrice Baldwin
Imagine That... by Stephen Bowkett
Self-Intelligence by Stephen Bowkett
StoryMaker Catch Pack by Stephen Bowkett

EFFECTIVE LEARNING & LEADERSHIP

Effective Heads of Department by Phil Jones & Nick Sparks
Leading the Learning School by Colin Weatherley
Closing the Learning Gap by Mike Hughes
Strategies for Closing the Learning Gap by Mike Hughes with Andy Vass
Transforming Teaching & Learning by Colin Weatherley with Bruce Bonney, John Kerr & Jo Morrison
Effective Learning Activities by Chris Dickinson
Tweak to Transform by Mike Hughes
Making Pupil Data Powerful by Maggie Pringle & Tony Cobb
Raising Boys' Achievement by Jon Pickering
Effective Teachers by Tony Swainston
Effective Teachers in Primary Schools by Tony Swainston
Effective Leadership in Schools by Tony Swainston

EFFECTIVE PERSONNEL MANAGEMENT

The Well Teacher – management strategies for beating stress, promoting staff health & reducing absence
by Maureen Cooper
Managing Challenging People – dealing with staff conduct by Maureen Cooper & Bev Curtis
Managing Poor Performance – handling staff capability issues by Maureen Cooper & Bev Curtis
Managing Recruitment and Selection – appointing the best staff by Maureen Cooper & Bev Curtis
Managing Allegations Against Staff – personnel and child protection issues in schools
by Maureen Cooper & Bev Curtis
Managing Redundancies – dealing with reduction and reorganisation of staff by Maureen Cooper & Bev Curtis
Paying Staff in Schools – performance management and pay in schools by Bev Curtis

VISIONS OF EDUCATION SERIES

Discover Your Hidden Talents: The essential guide to lifelong learning by Bill Lucas
The Power of Diversity by Barbara Prashnig
The Brain's Behind It by Alistair Smith
Wise Up by Guy Claxton
The Unfinished Revolution by John Abbott & Terry Ryan
The Learning Revolution by Gordon Dryden & Jeannette Vos

EMOTIONAL INTELLIGENCE
Becoming Emotionally Intelligent by Catherine Corrie
Lend Us Your Ears by Rosemary Sage
Class Talk by Rosemary Sage
A World of Difference by Rosemary Sage
Best behaviour and Best behaviour FIRST AID by Peter Relf, Rod Hirst, Jan Richardson & Georgina Youdell
    Best behaviour FIRST AID also available separately

DISPLAY MATERIAL
Move It posters: Physical movement and learning by Alistair Smith
Bright Sparks by Alistair Smith
More Bright Sparks by Alistair Smith
Leading Learning by Alistair Smith

NEWLY QUALIFIED TEACHERS
Lessons are for Learning by Mike Hughes
Classroom Management by Philip Waterhouse & Chris Dickinson
Getting Started by Henry Liebling

SCHOOL GOVERNORS
Questions School Governors Ask by Joan Sallis
Basics for School Governors by Joan Sallis
The Effective School Governor by David Marriott (including audio tape)

For more information and ordering details, please consult our website www.networkpress.co.uk

Network Educational Press – much more than publishing...

NEP Conferences – Invigorate your teaching

Each term NEP runs a wide range of conferences on cutting edge issues in teaching and learning at venues around the UK. The emphasis is always highly practical. Regular presenters include some of our top-selling authors such as Sue Palmer, Barry Teare and Steve Bowkett. Dates and venues for our current programme of conferences can be found on our website www.networkpress.co.uk.

NEP online Learning Style Analysis – Find out how your students prefer to learn

Discovering what makes your students tick is the key to personalizing learning. NEP's Learning Style Analysis is a 50-question online evaluation that can give an immediate and thorough learning profile for every student in your class. It reveals how, when and where they learn best, whether they are right brain or left brain dominant, analytic or holistic, whether they are strongly auditory, visual, kinaesthetic or tactile ... and a great deal more. And for teachers who'd like to take the next step, LSA enables you to create a whole-class profile for precision lesson planning.

Developed by The Creative Learning Company in New Zealand and based on the work of Learning Styles expert Barbara Prashnig, this powerful tool allows you to analyse your own and your students' learning preferences in a more detailed way than any other product we have ever seen. To find out more about Learning Style Analysis or to order profiles visit www.networkpress.co.uk/lsa.

Also available: *Teaching Style Analysis* and *Working Style Analysis.*

NEP's Critical Skills Programme – Teach your students skills for lifelong learning

The Critical Skills Programme puts pupils at the heart of learning, by providing the skills required to be successful in school and life. Classrooms are developed into effective learning environments, where pupils work collaboratively and feel safe enough to take 'learning risks'. Pupils have more ownership of their learning across the whole curriculum and are encouraged to develop not only subject knowledge but the fundamental skills of:

- problem solving
- creative thinking
- decision making
- communication
- management
- organization

- leadership
- self-direction
- quality working
- collaboration
- enterprise
- community involvement

"The Critical Skills Programme... energizes students to think in an enterprising way. CSP gets students to think for themselves, solve problems in teams, think outside the box, to work in a structured manner. CSP is the ideal way to forge an enterprising student culture."

Rick Lee, Deputy Director, Barrow Community Learning Partnership

To find out more about CSP training visit the Critical Skills Programme website at www.criticalskills.co.uk